What the Economy Needs Now

What the Economy Needs Now

Edited by
Abhijit Banerjee, Gita Gopinath,
Raghuram Rajan and
Mihir S. Sharma

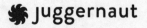

JUGGERNAUT BOOKS
KS House, 118 Shahpur Jat, New Delhi 110049, India

First published by Juggernaut Books 2019

10 9 8 7 6 5 4 3 2 1

P-ISBN: 9789353450311
E-ISBN: 9789353450335

Typeset in Adobe Caslon Pro by R. Ajith Kumar, Noida

Printed at Manipal Technologies Limited

Contents

How to Read This Book

The fourteen chapters in this book contain individual notes from thirteen economists. Each of these notes addresses one particular economic issue or sector that needs attention from the government. These notes represent the economists' own views, not that of any party or institution.

Some of the papers analyse these problems in considerable detail. So, to make it easier for all readers, the editors have provided a brief statement of the problems that need to be addressed before each paper discusses them in depth. In addition, each chapter ends with a summary of the suggested solutions.

The introduction, 'Why Strong, Equitable and Sustainable Growth Is Vital for India', serves also as an overview of the agenda we propose.

Finally, there is an afterword that identifies eight particular reforms to deal with the eight biggest challenges India faces.

Why Strong, Equitable and Sustainable Growth Is Vital for India

India is one of the fastest growing large economies in the world, having grown at an average of almost 7 per cent for the last twenty-five years. There have been many notable reforms over this period – most recently, the cooperative fiscal federalism that brought the goods and services tax (GST) into being; the enactment of the Indian Bankruptcy Code; and the dramatic dis-inflation of recent years, partly as a result of a move to an inflation targeting regime.

While all of this is commendable, we should not be satisfied with this. India is still one of the poorest countries in the G-20, and poor countries ought to grow faster because catch-up growth is easier. Also, the benefits of growth in India have been distributed extremely unequally, with top incomes rising much faster than the rest. We have seen new environmental challenges in the form of sharp increases in both local pollution levels and carbon dioxide emissions that, if unchecked, threaten to stall or reverse progress.

India is also not creating enough jobs: even though data on employment in India are both low quality and controversial, the recent news that 28 million applied for 90,000 low-level railway jobs suggests we are not satisfying the demand for jobs (Singh 2018). Unfortunately, we are not well-positioned to follow the export-led growth path that allowed many Asian countries to climb out of poverty. Despite abundant cheap labour, we are not part of many global supply chains. Even as global firms seek to diversify away from China so as to reduce political risk, India is rarely seen as an obvious alternative.

Given India's continental size, it need not follow the export-led path. It will, however, have to ensure that growth generates jobs and incomes across the skill spectrum, in the process:

- **Creating semi-skilled jobs** for those currently underemployed or unemployed and those who are seeking to leave low-productivity agriculture – even while enhancing the productivity of agriculture itself and the earnings of the agriculture-dependent population.
- **Increasing labour participation of women**. India has one of the lowest female participation rates in the labour force, down from 35 per cent in 1990 to 27 per cent in 2017. It is one of the few countries where this ratio has fallen. This limits the talent pool that the economy can draw upon, even as it constrains the life choices of women, many of whom, the evidence suggests, would like to be working.
- **Spreading jobs and economic development** from the coastal states to the interior, as well as to Kashmir and the North-Eastern states.

There are tremendous possibilities for reforms that will take us towards faster and more equitable growth, as this report will lay out. However, we have to **allocate scarce resources carefully to make sure that there is enough investment in sectors such as infrastructure to create jobs.** India's aggregate fiscal deficit (state plus Centre) is still close to 6.5 per cent of GDP, higher than almost any in the G-20, and not significantly lower than levels that existed five years ago. However, our investment rate has fallen sharply in recent years. Despite that, our external financing requirement (as measured by the current account deficit, or CAD) increased appreciably in early 2019, increasing vulnerability. Moreover, to the extent that India grows while being more reliant on domestic demand than were other Asian emerging markets, it needs a much greater focus on macroeconomic stability than they did. For all these reasons, it needs to **prioritize government spending better,** focusing on filling clear investment gaps and protecting the vulnerable. It also needs to increase revenues by **making the tax system more progressive** both in taxes levied and through more effective collection from rich non-payers, by bringing more people into the tax net and by charging users for government services where appropriate.

A key factor in spurring growth will be reforms that alleviate 'supply side' constraints on growth and job creation. We have to enable both the industrial sector and the service sector to operate at larger scale. This involves embracing **highly overdue labour reforms** including allowing for a rich menu of contracts with workers that allows for more possibilities than just permanent workers and short-term contractual labour in firms. Such additional contracting possibilities could give workers more job security, give firms the incentive to train and invest in their skilling, even as it gives firms more reason to scale up. Similarly, **cleaner title to land,** as well as a land acquisition process that protects the seller while simplifying acquisition, will reduce the cost of developing land, a critical need if we are to create jobs. A more predictable and smoother regulatory environment – which prunes redundant or unnecessary regulation, carefully sets regulations in new areas necessitated by our development and enforces regulations effectively and impartially – will create a much better environment for business. We must also improve the capabilities as well as strengthen the independence of our regulatory institutions.

Scale is also key for productivity growth which, in turn, is essential for India to expand its share of world exports. The ongoing reorientation of the United States away from dependence on China provides India with a great opportunity to position itself as a viable alternative for cheap sourcing of goods and parts. But this would require macro and industrial policy reforms of the kind outlined above, which **remove existing impediments to India becoming a valued partner in global supply chains.** Rolling back the recent increases in import tariffs, along with a renewed commitment to resisting protectionist policies, would be a good way of signalling this goal.

In outlining an economic agenda, we have to recognize that government capacity is limited – the number of government employees is often low relative to the tasks they are assigned. This is often compounded by low staff motivation and relatedly high absenteeism, as well as inadequate training. **Government takes on too much, while**

delivering too little. Yet, for growth to be equitable, a must in our democracy, effective and well-targeted government engagement is essential.

One partial solution is more decentralization, with more powers and funding delegated to the states, and, perhaps more importantly, within the states to **municipalities and panchayats.** It will allow for a much more dynamic decision-making process, resulting in government policies that are more sensitive to local conditions as well as more local democratic control of officialdom.

The strategic use of technology has the potential to help here – as long as we are careful not to make a fetish of technology, are mindful of the human dimension of transactions and deploy technology with enough safeguards. Technology can make it easier to monitor flows of funds and uses of funding locally, allowing for more devolution of funding, something that has been proposed by previous Finance Commissions. More generally, **effective use of technology can help substitute for government manpower,** increase the points of access to government services, help monitor service provision and reduce leakage in the system.

The debate on whether the public sector should occupy areas that can be serviced by the private sector will no doubt continue, and there is an obvious case for exiting areas where the public sector contributes little while draining the exchequer and distorting competition. The government should also reconsider its interventions in areas where it adds noise and uncertainty. For instance, the constant fiddling with agricultural import tariffs, the unpredictable closure or opening of export and import windows and the inability to procure agricultural commodities or release them effectively do significantly more damage than good to agriculture. While actions are taken in the name of the farmer or the consumer, it is the middleman who often benefits.

Moreover, even **when the consumer benefits from high farm production and low agricultural prices, which also help contain inflation, the cost to farmers can be significant.** The case of pulses is revealing. In 2016–17, for example, India witnessed its highest ever domestic production – close to 23 million metric tonnes – likely reflecting a combination of a normal monsoon after successive droughts and the farmer response to higher market prices and minimum support prices (MSPs). This was sufficient to fully satisfy domestic demand. Despite that, India imported a hefty 6.6 million tonnes of pulses (almost a third of total domestic production) at zero import duty – leading to a massive domestic supply glut and a sharp and sustained fall in prices of pulses over the next two years, which continues to this day, with prices currently 30 per cent lower than their 2016 peaks.

In addition to getting the government out of areas it should not be in, there is an equally urgent task: strengthening the government in areas where it does poorly or is virtually absent. These include regulating and certifying educational or medical service providers; apprehending and successfully prosecuting economic offenders; and regulating haphazard development and environmental despoliation without blocking growth.

For growth to be equitable and sustained, we have to reform our education, skilling, healthcare and welfare systems significantly. Our record on primary education is dismal, with **only about half of the children in class five**

able to do maths or reading at the class-two level. Parents have responded by increasingly migrating their children to private schooling, but private schools are only slightly better than government schools, and in their current form will not solve the problem of low education quality. It does not get better at higher grades – our scores in the Program for International Student Assessment (PISA) exams were so low that we refused to participate again in that international benchmarking exercise. The **poor quality of human capital may already be constraining growth** (industry is increasingly concerned about the large and growing skill deficit) and limits its inclusiveness and may prompt a premature move to replace workers with machines.

Healthcare is another area of major concern. In particular, the **public system has largely been abandoned by those patients who are seeking regular primary care.** They prefer paying for private treatment – even though many practitioners are unqualified and prescribe the wrong treatment in more than 70 per cent of the cases. This is partly a consequence of the failure of the public sector: public sector practitioners are often absent, and when present they put very little effort into treatment. This is especially worrying because dealing with the large, growing burden of non-communicable diseases (NCDs) and the many, only partly solved, child and maternal health issues would need front line providers to lead the charge. It is unclear how the recent Ayushman Bharat insurance scheme, which is the main current effort to deal with healthcare issues, will address these problems.

Similar concerns apply in the education sector. A **failure to ensure high-quality education and healthcare provision**

means that a substantial proportion of our future labour force will grow up underequipped with skills needed in the labour market and suffering from the long-term consequences of stunting and wasting. Much of the middle-aged population will be dealing with debilitating diseases that could have been prevented or controlled. This obviously limits the sustainability and the inclusiveness of growth.

The environment is, of course, a critical challenge to the continuation of our growth and to the extent to which growth translates into improved quality of life. Many of our cities are increasingly experiencing levels of pollution that border on the toxic. If we cannot manage the environment at our present level of development, greater growth will make matters far worse. The consequences of environmentally myopic policies are reflected, for example, in the **rapidly falling water table** in many parts of the country, which threatens the sustainability of our agriculture. Relatedly, climate change has already had significant effects on productivity and the quality of life in India and we need to be at the forefront of global efforts to combat it.

That our current policies do not add up to an inclusive and sustainable growth agenda is reflected in growing agitation across our society. Agrarian unrest, with the accompanying constant demand for farm loan waivers, is now compounded by demands for some form of government support from sections of society that are nowhere near the poorest. This reflects Indians' growing anxiety about their future and that of their children in an increasingly winner-take-all society, where they often end up on the losing side. Our welfare schemes like the Mahatma Gandhi National

Rural Employment Guarantee Scheme (MGNREGS) and Pradhan Mantri Gramin Awas Yojana are mostly directed towards the very poor (the one exception being the public distribution system [PDS]), so they do not serve the purpose of protecting those outside that group. **Without stronger, sustainable and inclusive growth we simply do not have the resources to expand our welfare schemes significantly,** but if we do generate that growth, not only will there be less demand for welfare but there will be more resources to service any demand.

The bottom line is that while we have performed creditably in the last twenty-five years across different administrations, there is no room for complacency given our economic challenges. They are mounting.

We are a group of economists, each with different specializations and interests, who have come together to offer proposals for the way ahead. Some of us are based in India, some outside, but we are all closely engaged in, and concerned about, India's development. We do not belong to any party, nor are we from the government. We hope this non-partisan analysis of our situation, while not intended to be comprehensive, will help spur debate as India moves to elections.

The rest of this introduction summarizes our proposals and offers our consensus view on some key issues we face. Individual notes by members of the group offer more details of individual views and proposals; each reflects the view of the author(s) in their personal capacity and does not necessarily represent the institution they are affiliated with.

Macroeconomic stability: A prerequisite to sustainable growth and job creation

India's economic history demonstrates over and over again the same lesson: preserving and protecting macroeconomic stability is an essential prerequisite to strong and sustained growth. **Every time macro stability has been traded off to boost growth, the economy has been pushed towards a crisis,** the consequences of which have undermined the very growth that was the initial policy focus.

Ensuring macroeconomic stability has at least three elements to it: maintaining low and stable inflation; ensuring the consolidated fiscal deficit leaves enough space for private investment; and ensuring that the CAD is sustainable and can be financed largely through stable capital inflows, to help insulate the economy from sudden swings in global sentiment.

High and variable inflation constitutes a regressive tax, with the poor bearing the biggest brunt, since their incomes are typically least indexed to inflation. It also dissuades foreign investors from investing in rupee assets. Similarly, large and unsustainable fiscal/external imbalances impart significant macroeconomic and financial market uncertainty, push up borrowing costs and risk premia in the economy and threaten financial stability. All this impedes private and public investment.

Fiscal consolidation to create space for more investment

The economy has made significant progress in combating inflation in recent years. Over the last four years (2014–18) inflation has averaged just over 4 per cent, versus almost 10 per cent in the previous five years, and household inflation expectations are getting progressively anchored. The same, however, cannot be said of the fiscal side. While the Centre's fiscal deficit has been steadily brought down, the combined deficit of the states – even after adjusting for the Ujwal DISCOM Assurance Yojana that saw states take on some of their power utilities' debt – has continued to widen in recent years. This increase has largely undone the Centre's consolidation. Consequently, the consolidated fiscal deficit, of both the Centre and the states, stood above 6.5 per cent of GDP in 2017–18 – not very different from its levels five years ago.

Our primary suggestions to make progress on this difficult issue are to:

- Stick to the path laid out by the Fiscal Responsibility and Budget Management (FRBM) Review Committee such that the **consolidated fiscal deficit is brought down to 5 per cent of GDP** and general government debt to 60 per cent of GDP.
- Formulate a 'grand bargain' between the Centre and the states, **giving states incentives to be aligned with the Centre's fiscal goals,** which is currently almost entirely missing:
  - Use the model of the GST Council as a successful example of cooperative fiscal federalism.
  - Use Finance Commission awards to reward good behaviour.
  - Gradually remove Central guarantees for the market borrowings of the states that go beyond pre-specified limits so that a state faces market borrowing costs that are correlated with its fiscal performance.

- **Adopt better accounting** for contingent and off-balance-sheet liabilities of the states and the Centre so as to estimate overall government financing needs, and therefore its claim on savings. This is especially important when we add the necessary healthcare and pension schemes that will last well into the future. Such entitlements have to be costed based on long-term usage and growth, not on current costs, especially since entitlements are virtually impossible to withdraw.

Reduce risks from the external sector

India's **heavy dependence on oil imports often results in 'boom–bust' cycles** on the balance of payments (BoP) when crude prices change. For example, the CAD narrowed to 0.7 per cent of GDP in 2016–17 as crude prices fell and was then tracking close to 3 per cent of GDP in 2018 when crude prices bounced back up. This resulted in a large BoP surplus in the first instance and a large deficit in the second. These sharp swings complicate monetary policy, as well as exchange rate and liquidity management, and create undue external and fiscal volatility (since oil prices also alter the fiscal maths). We should:

- Undertake a systematic programme to **hedge global crude prices**, as Panama, Ghana and Mexico have begun to do.
- Adopt a set of steps to **de-risk the external sector** by:
  - Attracting more foreign direct investment (FDI).
  - Dis-incentivizing 'hot money'.
  - Encouraging more hedging of foreign currency borrowing by firms.

- Developing domestic substitute financial assets linked to gold prices.

Fixing the stressed sectors

Careful but quick policy reforms are needed for the sectors/areas that are stressed. These include agriculture, infrastructure (including power), exports and banking. There are common themes in any revival. Typically, we need to **redeploy government effort in each of these sectors, focusing it on areas where it is truly needed** to play an enabling role. Excessive or misplaced bureaucracy and intervention result in inadequate access to markets, distorted prices and poor incentives. Whereas the recent focus on improving India's ranking on the World Bank's 'Ease of Doing Business' measures is commendable, we should guard against the temptation to focus on the specifics of the World Bank measures, while neglecting the broader impediments to producing in India. We now consider each of these sectors in more detail.

Agriculture and the rural economy

We need deep-rooted transformation of agriculture, treating it not as a sector that has to be propped up through repeated sops, but as an engine of India's job creation and growth. For that, it is imperative that we thoroughly reform agricultural and land policies. A key source of agrarian distress in recent years has been that the terms of trade confronting farmers have turned progressively more adverse, partly as a result of policies to combat food inflation. **While low inflation is**

desirable in itself, the impact on farmers also needs to be taken into account. A policy priority should be to reduce distortions in farm product prices as well as in input prices. Another important enabler is technology, both in educating and informing farmers and in opening access to markets. Some specific proposals to transform agriculture are:

- Increase investment in **research** – covering new seeds including those that have been genetically modified (GM), and the latest farming and irrigation techniques – and disseminate new techniques widely, including through digital means. Invest in infrastructure such as **irrigation, roads and improved transport and storage logistics.** Eschew loan waivers that divert resources from needed investment.
- Ensure that farmers receive more of what is paid by the consumer by:
  - Improving **farmer access to domestic and international markets** by reducing fees and restrictions on competition and building the necessary infrastructure.
  - Eschewing frequent closing or opening of access to international markets.
- Facilitate farming at scale for relevant crops:
  - Through the creation of farmer/producer cooperatives.
  - By enabling easier long-term leasing of land; ensuring landowners have clear title to their land is an important prerequisite.
- Move to a fixed cash subsidy per acre cultivated based on digitizing and identifying plots (as demonstrated successfully by the Rythu Bandhu scheme of the Telangana government).

- **Replace price support schemes** that are costly (because of corruption and inefficiencies in procurement and storage), ineffective (because procurement is not widespread, especially when and where most needed) and distortionary (because the wrong crops are incentivized).

• Improve and expand the current Pradhan Mantri Fasal Bima Yojana (PMFBY), especially as the climate gets more volatile.

 - Here **quick assessment of crop damage** using new technologies such as satellite images and drones, as well as quick payout into bank accounts, will increase the number of farmers who adopt this insurance scheme.

• For landless labourers, the best short-term policy option is likely to be to strengthen the NREGS. Evidence suggests places with well-implemented NREGS have significantly higher market wages – without hurting employment. Thus, increasing allocations to, and ensuring better implementation of, NREGS may be the best immediate policy option to protect the landless rural poor.

 - **Efficiency of NREGS spending** can be increased by working with line departments to improve asset quality and create better quality rural infrastructure.

Infrastructure

Accelerating the pace of infrastructure buildout will help in a number of ways. It will create jobs in construction and new economic activity around the resulting roads, ports, airports, railways and housing; it will promote inclusion as it connects interior rural areas to markets; it will make our exports (and import-competing manufacturing) more competitive as it reduces input costs such as land (as cheaper areas are connected) and power and improves logistics and reduces transportation costs; and it will open up India to both domestic and foreign tourism, which can be a tremendous source of semi-skilled jobs.

For this acceleration to happen, we must:

- **Untangle stalled projects** through continued efforts to improve the land acquisition process, while addressing environmental clearance issues, improving raw material availability and establishing various sector regulators.

- Improve access to land for development, through **computerized land mapping**; government-guaranteed titling; the creation of land banks; the use of auctions for land acquisition; and so on. Some states have had much success in these while others have lagged behind. The model of the GST Council can be used for sharing best practices between the Centre and the states, as well as for formulating national actions such as land titling reform.

- Free up public resources for investment through public finance reforms (asset recycling, asset swaps, expenditure reform).

- Revitalize public–private partnerships (PPPs) with appropriate and enforceable risk allocation.

- Create **special economic zones** (SEZs), not necessarily with the focus only on exports, but also for domestic production. Improved infrastructure and access to land and environmental clearances in such zones can accelerate investment. These can also be 'laboratories' for some experimentation with alternative regulations before there is a decision to scale them up. It is important, however, that the SEZs do not degenerate again into opportunities for land-grabbing and rent-seeking.

Power

Despite having some of the largest reserves of coal and substantial unutilized power generation capacity, India is short of both coal and power. This is the result of policy self-goals, arising from the dominant presence of government in coal mining and power distribution as well as from populist impulses in pricing. Nevertheless, our low base allows us to choose a path that is more energy-efficient as well as less polluting as we reform the system for the twenty-first century. For this we must:

- Free energy pricing to generate more exploration, especially for cleaner gas, while using **carbon taxes** (or tradable carbon use permits) to align private incentives and social costs.
- Expand participation in **auctions of mining rights** for coal.
- Allow more competition in allocation of natural gas blocks and exploitation of natural gas resources.
- Improve **access and reliability of the power grid** so that the use of inefficient diesel generators is reduced.
- Reform distribution by creating **competition for state monopolies.**
- Integrate **renewables** into power production, recognizing there will be a need for additional balancing power and storage.

Exports

India's non-oil, non-gold current account has deteriorated by almost 3 per cent of GDP in the last three years, which calls for urgent steps to improve the underlying competitiveness of the tradable sector. Boosting exports should be the linchpin of that strategy. The existing constraints in the export sector appear to be reflective of more general problems in manufacturing: low scale of production, low productivity, bureaucratic impediments and the high cost of inputs like land and power. In addition to our earlier suggestions to address these, we need:

• Trade agreements, simpler documentation procedures at ports and low and stable tariffs so that we can be part of global supply chains. High tariffs and other **impediments to cross-border trade** not only hamper domestic exporters but will also discourage foreign manufacturers from seeing India as a viable part of their supply chains.

Financial sector

Given the non-performing asset (NPA) buildup in the banking system, it is imperative we make the banking system more robust and well capitalized, expand its capacity to extend credit and improve its incentives to lend to the most productive sectors. While the recent travails of non-bank financial companies (NBFCs) are a matter of concern, some of their problems stem from an overly rapid expansion of their balance sheets as they grew to substitute for banks. Stability in the banking system will help spread stability to other parts of the financial system as, of course, will the reverse.

The main challenges for the banking sector are to **improve governance, transparency and incentives throughout the system**. Key measures should include:

- Cleaning up bank balance sheets by **reviving projects** that can be revived after restructuring debt.
- Improving governance and management at the public sector banks and then recapitalizing them.
- De-risking banking by encouraging the transfer or some risk-taking to non-banks and the market.
- **Reducing the number and weight of government mandates for public sector banks,** and banks more generally.

The non-bank financial sector needs a strong banking system as well as deep equity and bond markets, supported by liquid secondary markets and robust regulatory and legal infrastructure. Key priorities include:

- Developing **a liquid and deep corporate bond market** through policies to encourage institutional investor participation.
- Enhancing liquidity in the government debt market and making it more attractive to institutional and retail investors.
- Developing missing (or nascent) markets like fixed income derivatives to hedge the credit and interest rate risk of fixed income securities.

Making growth inclusive and sustainable

A good job is often the most important instrument of inclusion. We need to help individuals obtain the human capabilities that will enable them to secure and hold that job, and protect those who cannot get jobs. We now turn to proposals on inclusion.

Education

The single greatest limitation of the Indian education system is its inability to deliver universal functional literacy and numeracy at the primary school level. Several studies show that students who fail to achieve basic skills by the end of class three learn very little in subsequent years even if they are enrolled in school. Our top education policy priority is therefore:

- **A national mission to achieve universal functional literacy and numeracy by class three.** Key elements of delivering on this mission should include:
  - Improving incentives of existing teachers to attend and teach well.
  - Providing districts/schools with resources to hire supplemental tutors/utilize new technologies that will provide **small-group instruction** to students so that they can be taught at the right level.
  - Independent measurement of learning outcomes with rewards/recognition to states/districts/blocks/schools based on improvements in learning.

The Right to Education (RTE) Act's input-based approach to education quality was unlikely to succeed given the extensive evidence that most school inputs are neither necessary nor sufficient for improving learning outcomes. **RTE has led to an unnecessary and disruptive closure of several low-cost private schools** that parents were choosing of their own accord. In many cases, even government schools are in violation of these input-based norms. We therefore recommend:

- Repealing all input-based mandates for schools under RTE (for both public and private schools) and focusing instead on **regulation of private schools based on transparency and disclosure**. Such an approach will reverse current trends and instead facilitate:
  - The expansion of quality private school providers.
  - Localized, cost-effective innovations by government schools, which may be made difficult by RTE (such as hiring tutors without formal teaching credentials for providing supplemental instructional support).
- Finally, since school education is mainly in the domain of state governments, we recommend that the Union Ministry for Human Resource Development seriously implement the School Education Quality Index (SEQI) initiative established by the NITI Aayog. Implementing the SEQI consistently, and tying some Central funding to the extent of improvement in these indicators over time will help to:
  - Shift the **policy focus to outcomes** rather than inputs and programmes.
  - Encourage state-led innovation in cost-effective policies to improve outcomes.
  - Facilitate documentation and sharing of best practices across states.

While improvement in schooling is a key building block to education, we cannot neglect either vocational training/skilling or college education. Both will be critical to providing our youth with the wherewithal for the jobs of the future. **High-quality research universities** will be essential, both to train teachers for our colleges and to fuel the innovation needed for the next stage of our growth.

Dealing with the skills shortage

There is wide recognition that the current models of publicly subsidized skilling are not performing very well even though skills are extremely scarce. What seems to work better is the skilling provided by private firms that are training their own labour force. However, under current laws, firms can employ workers for up to one year, after which they either have to fire them or make them permanent. Since there are significant costs and inflexibilities in making workers permanent, many firms keep workers on short contracts and terminate them before they can become permanent. This state of affairs serves neither the firm, which has to hire new workers frequently and has no incentive to train them, nor the worker, who has no security of employment, and who is not trained.

At the same time, since the government is often the only employer that offers secure jobs, young people spend their twenties applying for these jobs rather than working. However, these jobs are extremely expensive – thanks partly to the munificence of successive Pay Commissions – and therefore there are too few of them. As a result, a cynic could argue that the **government and the private sector**

lack manpower, while young people sit at home filling applications and preparing for tests. We propose that:

- The law be amended to allow for multi-year fixed-term labour contracts, renewable when they end. Severance payments should increase steadily with duration of tenure. The intent would be to **move more contract labour into these fixed-term contracts.** These will protect labour better, both initially and over time, and give business some flexibility, as well as greater incentives to invest in training labour.

- We study why PPPs have in general not been a success in skilling. We also identify and share best practices that have worked. In particular, it is worth exploring whether it works better to **get firms to expand their existing training programmes to include trainees they will not necessarily hire,** since these training programmes clearly provide useful skills – rather than relying on stand-alone training firms.

- **Governments could set up paid internships** for those under twenty-six to work as support staff in government departments in field or staff positions. Performance on these could be an eligibility requirement for applying for government jobs. This will both help relieve the manpower problem in government and generate on-the-job skilling.

Women's labour force participation

Regarding women's labour force participation, there are clearly both supply-side and demand-side issues. The supply of women in the workforce is lowered because of families that do not allow women to work, and because women feel disempowered. On the demand side, there is a lack of women-friendly jobs in the private sector – as well as clear and growing discrimination. Some useful first steps here:

- Greater representation of women in state and national legislatures, as well as in public administration, the judiciary and the police, has been shown to reduce bias against women and encourage families to invest in women as earning members.

- **Public safety** is an important issue for women, and increasing women in the police is a way to make women feel safer.

- Going beyond quotas, increasing awareness of the costs of not having more women in the workforce, as well as **behavioural change interventions targeted at both women and their families** to encourage women's work are also needed.

- Women-friendly policies in the private sector need to be encouraged but legislating that they will need to pay for childcare and maternity leave may just discourage employing women. Such initiatives need to be subsidized by public funds, at least until private firms start recognizing that they need women.

Healthcare

There is much to be done to reform the healthcare system in India. Increasingly, NCDs like heart disease, diabetes and cancer are much more prevalent, so healthcare needs to be reoriented to address these.

- Expand **public health outreach efforts to private sector providers including those without a medical degree.** Given that they provide most of the primary healthcare, they have the reach to transmit our public health interventions (immunization, exercise, testing). Studies in West Bengal suggest that training private sector health providers improves their performance (measured by sending them 'fake' patients) significantly. Based on that, West Bengal has already begun to train many thousands of private sector health providers. Overall, it might make sense to:
  - Develop a series of simple training interventions that help these practitioners improve the quality of the care they provide.
  - Create a set of **cell-phone-based checklists for treatment protocols** (along the lines that Atul Gawande has proposed for the United States but much more basic) for these practitioners to use to react to the common symptoms they face.
  - Introduce a simple test that allows the government to certify these practitioners as '**health extension workers**', delivering various public health interventions.
  - Enforce existing laws that prohibit these practitioners from dispensing high-potency antibiotics and steroids, and encourage referrals for cases where these may be warranted.
- Carry out public health campaigns to raise the awareness of NCDs, immunization and the dangers of overmedication. Recent evidence suggests that edutainment may be a very powerful device in this regard and should be used extensively.

- **Build a second district hospital in every district headquarters** outside the state capital. Once it is built and is operational, refurbish and modernize the existing district hospital and bring it up to acceptable standards. The current district hospital is typically overcrowded in part because it is the only section of the public system that works somewhat better, and in part because private alternatives are expensive. The second hospital will provide much-needed backup for the Ayushman Bharat Scheme if the private hospitals do not cooperate. They can also serve as centres for diagnosis and treatment of NCDs.

Environment

Even while business complains about the difficulty of getting environmental approvals, the quality of our environment leaves much to be desired. In addition, with climate change looming, we should be thinking in terms of reaching peak carbon emissions within the next decade or so – and then sharply reducing them. We thus need to get more professional about the environment and climate change, and more transparent about the regulatory process.

- A new environmental protection law should be enacted under which pollution regulation is delegated to a **fully independent regulator who is appointed for a five-year term and removable only by impeachment.** The regulatory agency must be funded automatically through a charge of a fraction of industry revenue. The regulator must be required to use the best available scientific and economic evidence to set pollution fees for pollutants (or inputs closely linked to pollutants) equal to the estimated monetary value of the harm that they cause, and must have the power to levy fines for non-compliance. In addition, the regulator may limit or ban some pollutants, and shut down industries that fail to comply. Revenue from fees and fines should go to the government to be used to compensate losers, finance pollution control and clean alternatives, or for the general budget, and should not go to the regulator.

- Policies that would improve energy pricing in the short term can include:
  - Setting Coal India prices at international parity.
  - **Price electricity at social marginal cost and then use revenues for fairer energy access** through, for instance, funding connections under Saubhagya (free of fixed costs) and giving fixed transfers to agricultural users.
  - A separate policy is needed for pollution from cooking and heating fires, which is responsible for a quarter of Indian air pollution. To enable cooking and heating with electricity, electricity bills for low-income households should be refunded up to a limit of 100 kWh per month (300 kWh per month in winter) and a public information campaign conducted via television and radio to explain the dangers of air pollution from cooking and heating fires. Incentive schemes to prevent burning of crop residue could also be worked out.
  - Adopt Euro fuel standards faster than at present.
- Long-term planning changes include **city design that seeks to increase public transport, micro electrical vehicles and cycling**. India should invest in rail, which

is easier to electrify than road transport. Building regulations should minimize artificial heating and cooling.

- Congestion pricing of city traffic by onboard GPS tracking should be mandatory, with revenues used to improve pavements and public transport. The municipality could compensate existing vehicle owners and drivers through a temporary refund of automobile use taxes.

Social protection

India has more than 400 separate social protection schemes. A vast majority of them are funded at very low levels and do very little. However, they absorb a considerable amount of bureaucratic capacity. And despite the wide variety of schemes available on paper, as the many protests make clear, people do not feel protected. While MGNREGS provides some support for the rural landless, most other relatively poor people have only the PDS to fall back on. This widespread feeling of insecurity is one reason that it is so difficult to remove any government scheme, however inefficient.

We clearly need to create a **reliable pipeline for providing compensation to losers, as we move towards a more rational system of social protection.** The direct benefits transfer (DBT) is a good starting point and building on it by being credible in compensating losers will be key. Specifically, we suggest:

- Going through the hundreds of schemes and getting rid of most of them, retaining a small number that are targeted at the most important forms of risk that people face.

- Moving beyond the cash vs kind debate by adopting a **choice-based approach** on an experimental basis. For example, we could give beneficiaries the choice of opting for a cash transfer instead of subsidized food through the PDS – instead of policymakers opting for one or the other. With mobile banking and the PDS being digitized with e-PoS machines to enable portability of benefits, such a choice-based approach is feasible.
- **Automatically indexing social protection programmes (such as pensions) to inflation** to ensure that their value is not eroded over time. This is especially important since recipients of social welfare pensions are among the most vulnerable.

Reference

Mahendra K. Singh, 2018, 'Over 2.8 Crore Apply for 90,000 Railway Jobs', *Times of India*, 31 March 2018, https://timesofindia.indiatimes.com/india/over-2-8-crore-apply-for-90000-railways-jobs/articleshow/ 63551672. cms

1

HEALTHCARE

The Problems

1. Ayushman Bharat, the new publicly funded universal insurance scheme, will be difficult to implement given that the government will have to decide and settle disputes about which treatment patients should receive and how much it would cost. The government does not yet have the capacity to make these decisions, and the court system would struggle to handle what would turn out to be a very large number of claims.

2. India faces a surge in non-communicable diseases like diabetes and cancer; poorly qualified health practitioners with no accountability also cause the spread of antibiotic resistance.

3. Particularly in North India, patients have largely turned to under-qualified or informal private providers of primary healthcare – partly because government primary healthcare centres are poorly staffed and under-equipped.

4. Public hospitals and community healthcare centres are generally overcrowded and under-resourced – patients are forced to use them because private secondary and tertiary care is expensive.

A Note on Healthcare

Abhijit Banerjee

The biggest news in health and healthcare is Pradhan Mantri Jan Arogya Yojana (PMJAY) or Ayushman Bharat, which is a publicly funded universal insurance scheme that mainly covers hospital care. The coverage of this scheme is generous and, if properly implemented, it will protect people from the often-devastating *economic consequences* of a serious illness or an accident.

The concern with this scheme is that it is not easy to implement. Rampant fraud led to the closure in Rajasthan of the Rashtriya Swasthya Bima Yojana (RSBY), the previous edition of a publicly funded insurance scheme. These issues have not been tackled explicitly, so the scheme may run into problems.

In particular the model's reliance on the trust model means that the government, as against insurance companies, has to adjudicate claims about the appropriate prices and treatments. For example, the government will have to set the right price (for that location) for each individual service provided and also make a list of exactly what services would be provided to patients with specific conditions. In other words, there will need to be a full catalogue which specifies exactly what the hospital does if someone is brought in with chest pain, and how much it will be paid for it. For example, for a particular patient would the trust pay for a stent (cheap) or a bypass (expensive)? And in each case how much would it pay?

There is also the problem of what to do when there is prima facie evidence that either unnecessary procedures were carried out or false diagnoses were made. Or when there are claims that patients are being forced to pay extra for services that they are supposed to receive for free. Would the patient know what she is entitled to and what goes beyond her entitlement? And how do you settle the dispute, given that there will typically be no hard evidence either way – did the patient demand something the government won't pay for, or was it imposed upon them? Relying on our already overburdened court system will not work except in the most egregious cases, so it has to be based on threats of exclusion from the system in the future. But not every disputed claim is illegitimate. Therefore, some judgement will need to be exercised, or else legitimate hospitals will not want to participate in the scheme. But who will provide that judgement?

In the United States, under Obamacare, these tasks are carried out by professionals who have a great deal of expertise in healthcare and healthcare costs and can therefore detect patterns that do not add up, and make credible arguments against dubious claims. So far there seems to be no awareness of this issue and no plan to hire very large numbers of professionals to manage the system (indeed, it is not at all clear where so many professionals would come from). There is the idea that hospitals will hire Ayushman Mitras to guide patients through the system, but it is not clear that they will have the right incentives (they are hospital employees, after all) or the right skills.

However, even if the scheme eventually works well, which we certainly hope, it is not clear that it will solve the main health challenges we face. We are still the economy with the largest number of malnourished in the world, despite some recent improvements. We are also facing a surge in NCDs like diabetes, blood pressure and cancer – in part because of ageing, in part because of the poisoned environment in many of our cities and in part because of various lifestyle issues (lack of exercise, bad diet and tobacco/alcohol use, for example). Finally, we face rising resistance to antibiotics, largely because of overuse.

The obvious way to deal with these issues is to make use of people's primary point of contact with the healthcare system – the person they regularly see for what they believe to be minor ailments. This is the person who can spot any worrying changes in the patient's health, do a quick check of their haemoglobin, blood pressure and blood sugar, or measure a child's height and weight, and encourage them to take the required action. They are often close enough to be able to check up on whether the patient did take the recommended action (or whether he or she continues to take their medicine), and to put pressure on them if not. They can also pass on useful public health messages, such as the importance of wearing sandals, immunizing children or not cooking in closed environments.

Here is where we have a huge problem. Ayushman Bharat does very little for primary healthcare. It has been announced that 1.5 lakh health and wellness centres will be set up, partly to deal with primary healthcare issues including NCDs – but, given the budgetary allocation of less than Rs 1 lakh per centre, this looks more like a very minor upgrading of the existing sub-centres and/or primary healthcare centres (PHCs). Similar and sometimes more ambitious upgrading, including the provision of some free medicines, has been attempted by a number of states in the past; but, for the most part, there has been no reversal of the trend towards wholesale exit from public healthcare, especially in North India.

There is now a substantial body of work that documents that, in many states, more than three-quarters of visits to primary care centres are to private providers – even though most of these providers have no medical qualification whatsoever. This is in part because the sub-centres are open intermittently and unpredictably, and doctors and nurses are often missing from the PHCs. In part, it may also reflect the lackadaisical attitude of doctors in the public system; Das, et al. (2016) report that doctors in the public sector, while well qualified, spend very little time with the patient and do not make much use of their superior training – except when they are acting as private physicians, when they perform much better. It seems unlikely that small investments in these sub-centres and PHCs will change all that; the patients will probably continue to stay away, and therefore using these as the basis of outreach for NCDs and other public health interventions probably has limited potential.

The obvious alternative is to make use of the informal providers who do have access to the patient population. It should certainly be recognized that they have the potential to be a public health hazard, especially because they abuse antibiotics and steroids – which contributes to rising resistance.

However, the policy response to this phenomenon has been mostly to declare these informal providers illegal and then to ignore their existence. This essentially deprives us of the primary tool for dealing with the very serious health problems that we are facing. We need to think of ways to integrate them better into the overall healthcare project and give them better incentives, which would be easier if they had something to lose. Based on this we suggest the following steps.

1. **Recognize and train informal healthcare providers.** A randomized control trial that was carried out in West Bengal (published in *Science*, 2016) shows that training private sector informal healthcare providers improves their performance (measured by sending them 'fake' patients) by a very significant amount. Based on that, West Bengal has already begun training many thousands of informal health providers.

2. **Develop a set of cell-phone-based checklists for treatment protocols** for these practitioners to use, to react to the common symptoms they face. This is similar to what Atul Gawande has proposed for the United States (but much more basic).

3. **Develop a simple test that allows the government to certify these practitioners as health extension workers.** Passing this test will allow them to deliver various public health interventions and perhaps be paid for participating in them. Moreover, evidence suggests that

the patients are aware of the value of such certification and trust those certified more.

4. **Recognize those who are certified as the front line of defence against NCDs and malnutrition.** Think of ways to reward those whose referral leads to the detection of a serious ailment.

5. **Enforce existing laws that make it impossible for these practitioners to dispense high-potency antibiotics and steroids.** This includes shutting down stores which violate the existing laws about who can prescribe what. At the same time, make it legal for informal providers to prescribe a range of less critical medicines, much like the nurses.

6. **Expand the number of MBBS doctors and trained nurses coming out of the system and consider introducing some other intermediate degrees for practising a limited range of healthcare.** This is the model we had before Independence and the one that many other countries have adopted.

In addition, it is not clear that the government should rely entirely on the private sector to deliver tertiary care within PMJAY. Conflicts over the appropriate payment for treatment and accusations of fraud in private sector providers is common in the United States. There are already complaints from the healthcare sector about the prices the Indian government is proposing, which might result in many hospitals opting out and others selectively refusing to deliver certain treatments (even if that is against the rules). Given all this, having a public sector alternative available gives the government bargaining power that it can use when needed. As it turns out, the upper tiers of the public healthcare system, the district hospitals and community health centres (CHCs) are much more used than the PHCs and sub-centres; indeed, patients are often spilling out of their wards into the corridors and public areas. One reason for this difference with primary care is no doubt the fact that while primary healthcare in the private sector is cheap (and the patients may not know just how low the quality can be), secondary and tertiary care are expensive. But the other is that there is care available – these hospitals, being in the district headquarters and larger towns, find it much easier to make sure that doctors and nurses actually show up to work, than do the sub-centres and the PHCs which are in villages.

PMJAY will probably relieve some of this pressure on these public hospitals. However, for the reasons we suggest in the previous paragraph it still makes sense for the government to try to simultaneously improve the delivery of secondary and tertiary care in the public sector. Given that public hospitals will be able to bill their patients to PMJAY, which gives the public hospitals stronger reasons to compete with the private sector, it is a natural moment to expand this part of the government system. Therefore, we recommend, for secondary and tertiary care:

- **Build a second district hospital in every district headquarters outside the state capital**. Once it is built and is operational, refurbish and modernize the existing district hospital and bring it to acceptable standards.

Finally, it is very difficult to improve healthcare substantially unless we get the customers to demand better care (to fear antibiotics, seek out tests, and so on). This has to be a priority for any government. This is our final recommendation:

- **Carry out public health campaigns to raise the awareness of NCDs, immunization and the dangers of overmedication.** Recent evidence suggests that entertainment education may be a very powerful device in this regard.

References

Abhijit Chowdhury, Jishnu Das, Rashmaan Hussain, and Abhijit Banerjee, 2016, 'The Impact of Training Informal Health Care Providers in India: A Randomized Controlled Trial', *Science*, 354(6308).

Jishnu Das, Alaka Holla, Aakash Mohpal, and Karthik Muralidharan, 2016, 'Quality and Accountability in Health Care Delivery: Audit-Study Evidence from Primary Care in India', *American Economic Review*, 106(12).

The Solutions

1. The government will have to recognize that informal providers of primary healthcare are not going anywhere and should instead find ways to train, test, certify and reward them. Medical education should also allow for 'intermediate' degrees that produce practitioners licensed to practise a limited range of healthcare.
2. To control antibiotic resistance, it will be necessary to crack down on practitioners who mis-prescribe antibiotics and steroids, and on the chemists that fill these illegal prescriptions.
3. A second district hospital should be built in every district headquarter to take the pressure off the existing one – which can then be given upgraded technology and facilities.
4. Public health campaigns should be carried out so that Indians in general are more aware of the dangers of overmedication – as well as of the need for immunization and the lifestyle changes needed to minimize non-communicable diseases like diabetes.

2

INFRASTRUCTURE

The Problems

1. India needs more and better infrastructure – power plants, highways and urban amenities – if it is to grow faster. But not enough money is being invested in building infrastructure.

2. Some of the money that is needed can come from taxes and other forms of government revenue. But most of it will have to come from the private sector. Unfortunately, the private sector is now unenthusiastic about investing in something as risky as infrastructure. Banks are also unwilling to lend.

3. Earlier attempts to involve the private sector, such as through PPPs, have run into trouble – sometimes the private partner asked for better terms, at other times the government was slow with approvals, and projects stalled.

4. The government will have to balance the need to build infrastructure, the limited amount of money it has and the difficulty of working with the private sector. How can it do that?

Slow Pace of Infrastructure Buildout: Concerns and Key Steps*

Pranjul Bhandari

India's large investment deficit is well known. The investment rate has fallen by about six percentage points since the highs of 2011–12. The Asian Development Bank estimates that over the next five years the gap between current and needed investment levels will be about 4 per cent of GDP ($112 billion) annually.[1] It further estimates that public finance reforms could generate additional revenues to bridge up to about 40 per cent of the gap. Money to bridge the 60 per cent or so that remains will have to come from the private sector.

In addition to increasing spending on infrastructure while maintaining macroeconomic stability – in other words, while keeping an eye on the deficit and inflation – the government can help incentivize private investment by speeding up the resolution of stalled projects and partnering with private investors (via PPPs). The government can also

---

* The author would like to thank Neelkanth Mishra for useful discussions and suggestions.
[1] See https://www.adb.org/sites/default/files/publication/227496/special-report-infrastructure.pdf

work to develop the corporate bond market for sustainable financing of infrastructure. Here are a few general and sector-specific recommendations.

Maintain macroeconomic stability

Keeping the macro house in order is the primary requirement for creating an environment that scales up investment.

- **Fiscal consolidation** is necessary to keep borrowing costs for private investors low and to ensure that the country has a healthy stock of savings to channelize into investments.[2]
- **Low inflation** ensures stable returns to investors – they have a clearer idea of what they are getting in return for their investment.
- We have found that policy uncertainty is a huge dampener for investment. **Well-articulated policy decisions** that bring in certainty and minimize surprises are necessary for private sector capital expenditure to grow and flourish.

Reform public finance

The government needs to scale up infrastructure spending, but in a fiscally responsible way, so that it remains sustainable. We recommend the following:

- **Switching government expenditure** from current expenditure, on such things as wages and salaries

---

[2] See Prachi Mishra's note in this volume, 'Responsible Growth: Way forward for India', for a discussion on a sustainable path for public debt and the fiscal deficit.

(running at 11.4 per cent of GDP presently), to capital (1.6 per cent of GDP), without abandoning the fiscal glide path. Targeting subsidies at those who really need them and weeding out sub-scale legacy expenditure schemes can lower the current expenditure bill.

- **Raising revenues** by removing the many exemptions and distortions in the current **GST** structure.
- **Swapping assets,** i.e., selling additional spectrum, disinvestment from the public sector and monetizing government landholdings, and using the proceeds to invest in new infrastructure projects. **Recycling capital** by selling/auctioning brownfield assets and allocating proceeds to finance greenfield infrastructure.[3]
- **Other innovations** include **land value capture,** a method by which the increase in property or land value due to public infrastructure improvements is captured through land-related taxes or other means to pay for the improvements.[4]
- Setting **user charges** for infrastructure services with greater regard to cost recovery will also help.

---

[3] This is already happening in road projects, where the government is transferring completed roads to the private sector (the toll–operate–transfer model) and using the resources to build new roads (the engineering–procurement–construction model). Completed projects can be sold to domestic and foreign institutional investors who have long-term liabilities but a limited appetite for risk.

[4] A variant of this was tried in the Hyderabad Metro project. The government leased adjoining land for commercial activity to Larsen and Toubro (L&T) for sixty years. Lessons from the experience of Japan, Korea and China can be useful here.

Untangle stalled projects

India's stock of stalled projects rose sharply from 2011 onward.[5] While they have moderated a notch from the highs, the 'stalling rate' for private capex projects remains elevated (at 24 per cent versus the long-term average of 13 per cent). Freeing up these projects is an important driver of new private sector capital expenditure.

One-third of the stalled projects are due to government policies.[6] We provide recommendations to address three main reasons of policy-related stalling:

• **Land acquisition:** Since the enactment of the 2013 Land Acquisition, Rehabilitation and Resettlement (LARR) Act, some states have explored innovative models of procuring land for infrastructure projects that don't invoke the LARR. Andhra Pradesh, for example, has pioneered the 'land pooling' model for the greenfield state capital Amaravati, where 25,000 farmers have voluntarily pooled 33,000 acres of land. By giving them an alternative form of compensation, in this case a share of the developed land, among other benefits, the state has made them direct stakeholders in the success of the

---

[5] Based on data from the capex database maintained by the Centre for Monitoring Indian Economy (CMIE). Stalling rate is defined as projects stalled as a percentage of projects under implementation.

[6] The remaining are due to market conditions, etc. We find that the twin balance sheet problem, weak world growth, increased policy uncertainty and lower expected future returns explained a large proportion of the capex slowdown (see Pranjul Bhandari and Dhiraj Nim, 'India's Investment Challenges: What Can Go Right', HSBC Global Research).

project. We recommend that such incentive-compatible models are codified and encouraged.[7]

- **Environmental clearance:** The incoming government should consider strengthening the institutional architecture for environmental regulation to ensure greater transparency and to enable decisions to be driven directly by the data. We recommend the establishment of an independent, professional environmental regulator, with adequate teeth and specialist expertise to appraise projects and monitor compliance.[8]

- **Raw material availability:** Lack of direct access to coal from mines – coal linkages – continues to be the biggest reason for policy-related stalling. Operationalization of the new Coal Mining Policy (which includes commercial miners) needs to be expedited.

Revitalize public–private partnerships

There is broad consensus that getting PPP models right is critical, and the lived experience of PPPs over the last two decades provides valuable lessons. We believe that it is time to revisit the governance and institutional architecture of PPPs in India. Our recommendations are to:

- Operationalize an **apex national-level entity** for institutional capacity building, research and analysis on

[7] For a detailed discussion, see Maitreesh Ghatak's note in this volume, 'Land Market Reforms'.

[8] A detailed blueprint for such an entity – a National Environmental Appraisal and Monitoring Authority (NEAMA) – was put together in 2011, and in 2015 the Supreme Court repeatedly asked the government to constitute such an authority.

PPPs in India ('a public–private partnership institute, or 3PI').[9]

- Establish **sector regulators** and 'best practice' design principles (governance, expertise, processes, etc.).
- Outline key principles for **risk allocation** in PPP contracts. Establish clear norms for **financial oversight of special purpose vehicles** (move to commercial audit from government audit, which is currently open for access under the Right to Information Act and Article 12 of the Constitution). Outline **clear norms for renegotiation of agreements.** Operationalize a robust but nimble dispute resolution mechanism.

Some sector-specific recommendations

- **Railways:** Embark on a step-wise freeing up of the railways. Establish an independent regulator which has the power to fix fares and goods tariff rates as well as fair access regulation, licensing and technical standards. Separate operations from the setting up of infrastructure.[10]

---

[9] The Kelkar Committee strongly endorses the '3PI' which can, in addition to functioning as a centre of excellence in PPPs, enable research, review, rollout activities to build capacity, and support more nuanced and sophisticated models of contracting and dispute redressal mechanisms. See 'Report of the Committee on Revisiting & Revitalising the PPP Model of Infrastructure Development Chaired by Dr. V. Kelkar', http://pib.nic.in/newsite/PrintRelease. aspx?relid=133954

[10] These recommendations are in line with the Bibek Debroy Committee report, 'Report of the Committee for the Mobilization of Resources for Major Railway Projects and Restructuring of Railway Ministry and Railway Board', http://www.indianrailways.gov.in/railwayboard/ uploads/directorate/HLSRC/FINAL_FILE_Final.pdf.

- **Roads:** Given the sheer number of roads and highways that need to be built or upgraded, different models need to coexist. The currently popular ones are toll–operate–transfer and the hybrid annuity model (HAM). A sector regulator (discussed under the PPPs section) will need to advise on the optimal mix of the different models.[11]

- **Power:** India will continue to need more power, and that means stronger attempts to reform the state electricity boards (SEBs) than has been attempted so far.[12] Further, as renewables become a larger share of power generation, the transmission grid will need to be redesigned appropriately.[13]

- **Urban infrastructure:** Incentivizing state governments to give more freedom to municipal bodies may be necessary. The 14th Finance Commission earmarked additional funds for municipal bodies, and that can be scaled up further over time. NITI Aayog's role can be expanded to disseminate best practices principles to cities.

Develop the corporate bond market

While banks will remain an important finance vehicle for investment, increased capital requirements (like Basel III)

---

[11] In a surge of ordering in recent times, many companies with weak balance sheets have won orders. They may not achieve financial closure easily and, consequently, specific sections of roads projects could get stuck.

[12] For more, see Prachi Mishra's note in this volume, 'Responsible Growth: Way forward for India'.

[13] For more, see Neelkanth Mishra's note 'Energy Reforms' in this volume.

and the inherent maturity mismatch related to long-term project lending implies bond financing must assume a greater role to complement banks.[14]

---

[14] For a detailed discussion on steps needed to develop the corporate bond market, see Eswar Prasad's note in this volume, 'Financial Sector Developments and Reforms'.

The Solutions

1. The government will have to make sure that the Indian economy looks attractive and stable – with low inflation, solid regulation and steady policies.
2. Some projects in the past ran into trouble because government clearances were slow or raw materials became unavailable. Ensure that does not happen again.
3. Don't abandon PPPs. Instead, increase the capacity in the government sector to manage these partnerships, and give these new regulators independence, funding, expertise and power.
4. Find other ways for households' savings to be channelled into infrastructure, besides banks. One way is to build up a market for corporate debt or bonds.

3

INDIA AND THE WORLD

The Problems

1. India's current account deficit – how much more it imports than it exports – is very sensitive to the global price of crude oil. When oil is expensive, the CAD is too high for comfort; when it falls, the CAD can look manageable.
2. Indian producers are not particularly competitive – which means that even when you take oil and gold imports out of the picture, exports are growing far less than are imports.
3. Any CAD has to be paid for by capital inflows into the economy. For stability, these should be long-term flows like FDI – but India depends too much instead on short-term 'hot money'.
4. When a country exports less than it imports, its currency depreciates – or loses value. But a lengthy and outsized depreciation of the rupee, while a natural consequence of a high CAD, would also stoke fears about macroeconomic instability.

De-Risking the External Sector

Sajjid Z. Chinoy

Abstract

The sharp decline in crude prices in late 2018 provided much-needed relief to India's external sector. But we must remain cognizant of underlying fault lines. The pressure on India's balance of payments through much of 2018 revealed: (i) India's external balances remain very sensitive to sharp swings in global crude prices, creating 'boom–bust' cycles on the external sector precipitated by crude price movements; (ii) the underlying (non-oil, non-gold) current account balance has deteriorated sharply in recent years and is contributing to the pressures; and (iii) there still exists an uncomfortably high reliance on volatile capital flows to fund the current account deficit.

Consequently, the policy focus must be to narrow the CAD to more sustainable levels – even if crude prices were to re-accelerate – and to de-risk the external sector more generally. This would entail: (i) narrowing the consolidated fiscal deficit (since the recent increase in the CAD simply reflects an incipient investment recovery against the backdrop of high public dis-saving); (ii) improving the competitiveness of the tradable sector (through infrastructure, factor market reforms, improved viability of small and medium enterprises [SMEs]) to improve the non-oil, non-gold current account balance; (iii) creating an institutional framework to systematically hedge sharp crude price movements to help mitigate external sector and fiscal risks; and (iv) continue working on creating an enabling domestic environment (regulatory, tax, ease of doing business) to attract more stable capital inflows (such as FDI and passive bond flows) so that the CAD can be increasingly financed by such inflows and less by volatile or pro-cyclical flows.

Context and challenge

- For much of 2018, India's external imbalances widened to levels that appeared unsustainable, particularly against an increasingly challenging global backdrop characterized by a continued normalization of financial conditions in some developed economies.

- India's CAD widened to 2.7 per cent of GDP in the first half of 2018–19 versus 1.9 per cent of GDP the previous year, and was on track to being close to 3 per cent of GDP in the second half of the year if oil had continued averaging $75/barrel.

- The collapse in crude prices has provided much-needed relief on the external front. But this should not mask underlying pressures: India's underlying (non-oil, non-gold) current account balance has deteriorated by almost 3 per cent of GDP in three years – suggestive of waning underlying competitiveness.

- On the capital account, the economy witnessed portfolio outflows for the first half of the (fiscal) year – precipitated by a tightening of global financial conditions – causing net capital inflows to slow significantly.
- The combination of a widening CAD and the sharp slowing of capital inflows meant the economy witnessed a meaningful BoP deficit in the first half.
- This resulted in a steady depletion of foreign exchange reserves and sustained rupee depreciation pressures. While some degree of rupee depreciation was an inevitable/optimal response to a negative terms of trade shock (emanating from higher crude prices), relentless and outsized rupee depreciation risks both: (i) engendering self-fulfilling pressures, and (ii) stoking financial and macroeconomic instability concerns.

What needs to be done?

While the sharp decline in crude oil prices recently has alleviated the stress, BoP pressures need to be addressed more fundamentally through a multipronged approach that: (i) reins in the CAD; (ii) reduces the susceptibility of the CAD to swings in global crude prices; (iii) improves the quality of capital inflows – such that a larger fraction of the CAD can be financed by stable flows; and (iv) continues augmenting foreign exchange reserves/buffers through bilateral and multilateral swap agreements.

Current account measures

A key policy imperative is to narrow the CAD to more sustainable levels. The experience over the last decade suggests a CAD in the range of 1.5–2.5 per cent of GDP can be financed predominantly by stable capital inflows (FDI and NRI deposits), thereby minimizing reliance on volatile or pro-cyclical sources of funding. Reining in the CAD would likely entail:

- **Bringing down the consolidated fiscal deficit, which is still close to 6.5 per cent of GDP.** At these levels, India's consolidated fiscal deficit remains an outlier in the emerging market universe. While the Union government has been steadily reducing its deficit, state deficits have doubled in the last five years and thereby largely undone the Centre's consolidation (see Figure 1). The CAD is simply the gap between investment and savings in the economy. The widening of the CAD therefore is simply reflecting an incipient pickup in domestic investment against the backdrop of high public dis-saving – in other words, a high consolidated fiscal deficit. Thus, the more the consolidated fiscal deficit can be brought down, the more the CAD can be compressed without having to

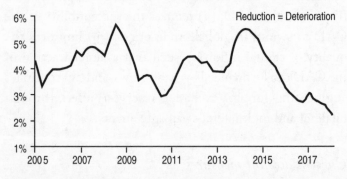

Figure 1: India's underlying current account surplus (excluding oil and gold) (four-quarter moving average, as a percentage of GDP)

Source: RBI, JP Morgan calculations

reduce investment or private consumption (so as to boost private savings). To achieve this, therefore:

– The Centre must assiduously follow the fiscal path laid out by the FRBM Review Committee to reduce its deficit to 2.5 per cent of GDP by 2022–23.

– State deficits must be reined in by changing the incentives under which state finances operate and better aligning incentives with desired outcomes. The 15th Finance Commission should perhaps consider: (i) designing their horizontal distribution formula to include incentives for states to be fiscally prudent; and (ii) suggest regulatory interventions to ensure state borrowing costs are correlated with underlying fiscal positions.

• **Improving tradable sector competitiveness.** A key source of external sector pressures is the sharp deterioration of the underlying (non-oil, non-gold) current account (by almost 3 per cent of GDP over the last three years), suggesting waning underlying competitiveness (see Figure 2). To improve the competitiveness of the tradable (both exports and import-competing) sector, policymakers must:

– Continue doubling down on infrastructure buildout (particularly transportation and port infrastructure) and continue with factor market reforms (land, labour, financial sector) to increase efficiencies, reduce costs and improve competitiveness of the tradable sector.[1]

---

[1] See Pranjul Bhandari's note, 'Slow Pace of Infrastructure Buildout', in this volume for a fuller discussion on the infrastructure sector prospects and constraints; and the note by Gita Gopinath and Amartya Lahiri, 'India's Exports', for policy initiatives to boost India's exports.

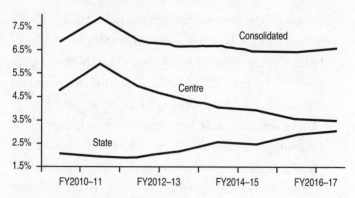

Figure 2: India's fiscal deficit (as a percentage of GDP)
Source: RBI

Perhaps these factor market reforms (land, labour) can first be tried in special export zones to reduce the political economy challenge.

– Improve the viability of the SME sector (a key labour-intensive, export and import-competing sector) and create an enabling environment (e.g., liberalizing labour laws) for SMEs to achieve scale economies.

– Address the tariff-inversion problem in several sectors by bringing down tariffs on intermediate imports in line with those on final goods.

– Formulate an overarching strategy to exploit the (quite large) untapped potential of agricultural exports by dismantling export controls and stockholding limits (Essential Commodities Act) that militate against scale economies.

- In this vein, policymaking must be nimble and stand ready to take advantage of Chinese tariffs on US agricultural products by quickly facilitating export of key agricultural products (cotton, soybean, maize) to China.

- Insulating the economy from sharp swings in crude prices by creating an institutional framework to systematically hedge crude prices.
  - India's heavy dependence on oil imports often results in boom–bust cycles on the BoP when crude prices swing around. For example, the CAD collapsed to 0.7 per cent of GDP in 2016–17 as crude prices fell and was then tracking close to 3 per cent of GDP in 2018 when crude prices bounced back up. This resulted in a large BoP surplus in the first instance and a large deficit in the second. These sharp swings complicate monetary, exchange rate and liquidity management, and create undue external and fiscal volatility (since changing oil prices also alters the fiscal maths).
  - Policymakers should smooth out this volatility by undertaking a systematic programme to hedge global crude prices, as some other economies have begun to do. This would significantly reduce external sector uncertainty and also impart more certainty to Budget projections. But doing so would entail creating a transparent and institutionalized framework to systematically hedge international crude prices so as to align bureaucratic incentives.
  - Hedging crude prices is not meant to second-guess future market movements; instead it is meant to mitigate risk and avoid boom–bust cycles. The government effectively used excise duty changes to ensure equitable burden sharing between the public and private sector of the oil windfall. Hedging crude prices would ensure less uncertainty/volatility of the terms of trade shock.

- Separately, authorities must be complimented for
  deregulating pump prices; this must be persisted with,
  because the volume response to price changes serves
  as an automatic stabilizer for the CAD.

Capital account measures and augmenting foreign exchange reserves

- Apart from reining in and smoothing the CAD, efforts
  must be undertaken to attract more stable capital inflows
  so that any given CAD is increasingly financed by stable
  inflows and is not reliant on volatile and pro-cyclical
  capital flows (portfolio investment/trade credits/banking
  capital).
  - Regulatory, tax, ease-of-doing business policies must
    combine to create a more enabling environment to
    attract more FDI, such that FDI flows are financing
    a progressively larger fraction of any CAD. Seventy
    per cent of the growth in China's exports to the
    United States in the last decade came from US
    firms manufacturing in China. FDI inflows that
    subsequently generate exports thereby simultaneously
    help the current and capital account, apart from
    facilitating technological transfer and boosting
    productivity.
  - Policymakers must also gradually prepare the
    groundwork to enter a global bond index, so the
    economy can eventually become the recipient of more
    'passive' debt inflows that are more sticky and less
    sensitive to changes in global sentiment.

- **Firms that are not naturally hedged must be induced/ incentivized/mandated to hedge any foreign currency borrowings** so as to avoid any systemic buildup of financial vulnerabilities, apart from not constraining the exchange rate as a policy instrument.
- **Policymakers must continue entering into more bilateral and multilateral swap engagements to boost 'effective' foreign exchange reserves** and augment the economy's buffers.

The Solutions

1. The government will have to commit to reducing its fiscal deficit – and to pushing states to reduce theirs. When the government spends more than it earns, it pushes up the CAD as well.

2. The tradable sector – both exporters and those Indian producers who compete with imports – has to become more competitive, so exports grow faster than imports and the CAD decreases. This would need more and better infrastructure, more flexible land and labour laws, and a focus on growing agricultural exports.

3. As long as India is a big oil importer, it will not be totally insulated from higher oil prices. But if there were better ways to reduce the uncertainty caused by sudden shifts in the oil price, you could at least ensure there was less instability. Institutions that allow companies and the government to hedge against changes in oil prices need to be built.

4. Another source of stability would be attracting long-term capital flows, such as FDI. This would again need the government to make investing in India look genuinely attractive.

4

WELFARE REFORM

The Problems

1. India's social protection – or 'welfare' – schemes are too many in number, and too inefficient.
2. Because of design problems and corruption, these schemes typically fail to sufficiently assist the poor who are their intended beneficiaries.
3. There is no consensus among politicians and activists on whether cash transfers can effectively replace schemes such as the public distribution system, which distributes food rations.
4. While the government will struggle to find the resources to introduce better-designed schemes without ending the older ones, shutting down existing schemes will create political discontent – so how can a government escape this trap?

Social Protection

Maitreesh Ghatak

There are hundreds of social protection schemes in India, from housing to food, from maternity benefits and child welfare to old-age support. Many of them are funded at very low levels that limit their effectiveness. While their performances across the country vary, it is broadly true that many of these schemes are beset with problems that make them less impactful than they could be.

First, there is the problem of eligibility. Often, those who should not be getting a benefit get it (inclusion errors), while those who should be getting it don't get it (exclusion errors).

Second, there is the problem of leakage, wastage and corruption in the delivery process.

Third, even if the implementation process were faultless – so that the first two problems were absent – administering these programmes uses up considerable manpower and resources.

Fourth, some of these schemes involve subsidies which distort the allocation of resources. For example, subsidies for water and electricity arguably cause environmental damage and supply-side problems (falling water tables and power blackouts). Moreover, they benefit the relatively better-off more than they do the poor – since the poor consume less of the relevant good or service. For example, power subsidies favour those who have access to electricity and, among them, those who consume more power.

Finally, leaving aside the problems on the delivery side listed above, there is also a basic problem that subsidies or in-kind transfers have – they do not leave the decision to the recipients as to what their specific needs are.

The core principles of reforming social safety net should be to:

- Reduce the number of schemes drastically to a manageable number, all of which are aimed at the most important risks. However, removing any scheme, however inefficient, will hurt some vulnerable group and so there has to be a concrete plan for compensation for losers in the process of reforming the social protection system, along the lines of the direct benefits transfer.

- Move beyond the cash vs kind debate in the context of some specific welfare programmes by focusing on beneficiary preferences and taking a *choice-based* approach. For example, in the context of food distribution through the PDS, we propose giving beneficiaries the choice of opting for a cash transfer, instead of policymakers deciding between the form of transfer (e.g., PDS and DBT). Muralidharan, et al. (2017) in their study on DBT in food found that preferences for it varied across beneficiaries depending on access to banking. For example, cash transfers work well if there is ready access to banking services as well as to markets, which is not true for remote rural areas. With mobile banking and the PDS being digitized with e-PoS machines to enable portability of benefits, such a choice-based approach has become feasible. This would also put pressure on PDS owners to stop diversion of their stock to the open market and to maintain the quality of the rations they supply. Also, as the study on DBT referred to above found, over time – as logistical problems are sorted out and people adapt to the new system – the acceptability of DBT to beneficiaries goes up. To minimize logistical problems, one should put in some reasonable restrictions on sticking to either the in-kind or cash transfer for a certain minimum period. There is also an issue of the entitlement of a family vs that of an individual. Under the PDS, the allocation is household-specific and so with a cash transfer opt-in, one would have to ensure that the family has claims to it.

- In general, we favour moving to uniform and universal cash transfers as much as possible. Cash transfers reduce administrative costs, corruption and various distortions involved with in-kind transfers. Evidence from low- and middle-income countries suggests that, on average, cash transfers to the poor do not cause them to work less or spend their money on inessential consumption, which are the usual concerns that are raised about cash transfers (see Banerjee, et al. 2017; Evans and Popova 2014). However, with the possibility of choice, there may be some scope for corruption, and so transparency regarding the implementation of the scheme is essential.

- Given the fiscal realities, we are restricting ourselves mainly to the forms of delivery of existing welfare schemes as opposed to proposing new schemes, such as a fully-fledged universal basic income scheme. However, we are not opposed to a general means-tested cash transfer scheme (as opposed to a universal or non-means-tested one) or schemes aimed at specific demographic groups (e.g., old-age pensions or maternity benefits), so long as the amounts involved are not too small. A key part of making such schemes effective would be an automatic indexation to inflation to ensure that their value is not eroded over time. This is especially important as these schemes are aimed at the most vulnerable sections of society.

References

Abhijit V. Banerjee, Rema Hanna, Gabriel E. Kreindler, and Benjamin A. Olken, 2017, 'Debunking the Stereotype of the Lazy Welfare Recipient: Evidence from Cash Transfer Programs', *The World Bank Research Observer*, 32(2): 155–84.

David K. Evans and Anna Popova, 2017, 'Cash Transfers and Temptation Goods', *Economic Development and Cultural Change*, 65(2): 189–221.

Karthik Muralidharan, Paul Niehaus, and Sandip Sukhtankar, 2017, 'Direct Benefits Transfer in Food: Results from One Year of Process Monitoring in Union Territories', Working Paper, University of California, San Diego.

The Solutions

1. The government should focus on ensuring that citizens' choice is at the centre of social protection schemes – for example, families should be allowed to choose for themselves whether they want their food ration in cash or in kind.
2. Any welfare reform that ends a particular social protection scheme should be accompanied by an attempt to directly compensate the 'losers' from the policy change.
3. Cash transfers in general give the recipients more control and are less prone to corruption.
4. Any new 'basic income' scheme, whether targeted at a specific group like farmers or more generally to the poor, must provide sufficient income – and the entitlement should be linked to inflation so that it goes up as prices increase.

5

A MARKET FOR LAND

The Problems

1. To build factories and towns, you need land. But, in India, acquiring land has become very difficult.
2. Farmers see their land as not just the source of their daily livelihood, but also as their only source of income security and wealth. If they lose their land, they rarely have the skills to work and earn anywhere else.
3. Sometimes it isn't even certain who owns a particular parcel of land – in many parts of India, land records are fragmented and disputed.
4. Recent policy changes meant to give farmers a better deal on their land give too much power to bureaucrats. A more localized, farmer-specific method is needed. What can the government do to persuade farmers to give up their land for projects?

Land Market Reforms[*]

Maitreesh Ghatak

Any large project that requires a substantial amount of land is difficult to implement in India because of high transaction costs. It is not just that land is scarce or that negotiating the right price is difficult. The problems run deeper: negotiating with thousands of farmers in a contiguous area, sifting through incomplete land records and settling disputes that move through courts at a very slow pace, all become serious constraints for industrial and infrastructure projects.

From the point of view of farmers, land is not merely an income-generating asset but a secure form of holding wealth, an insurance policy and a pension plan – all combined. Given that their skills are specific to agriculture, if they sell their land they will not have any other option but to work as unskilled labourers – which is not an attractive option in a labour-surplus economy. As a result, the true price of land is much higher than what would be dictated by current market prices. This has little to do with the relative

---

[*] The note draws on joint work with Parikshit Ghosh regarding the auction proposal and the critique of the LARR Act.

profitability of industry or agriculture or the physical scarcity of land. Rather, it is driven by the absence of good insurance mechanisms and financial instruments, and low levels of human capital, all of which make switching to alternative occupations costly for farmers.

The availability of land is a general problem that affects both the private and the public sector. For the public sector, the government has the option of utilizing the legal provisions of the Land Acquisition Act. In this context, the most glaring flaw in the 2013 Land Acquisition, Rehabilitation and Resettlement Act and the subsequent 2015 ordinance is that it takes a centralized and bureaucratic approach when it comes to determining the cost of a particular parcel of land. The arbitrary compensation formula is based on under-reported values and historical data, which do not reflect the ground realities that emerge after a major industrial or infrastructural project is launched. Multiplying the existing market price by two or four, as the LARR Act does, is simply a shot in the dark that has no guarantee of hitting the mark. Instead of relying on the discretion of politicians, bureaucrats and expert committees to put a price on valuable natural resources like land, minerals, natural gas and airwaves – which requires guesswork at best and leads to corruption at worst – the best way to put a price on a scarce resource is through greater reliance on economic mechanisms.

We outline some specific proposals below.

Auctions for acquiring land

The government should buy some land in and around the project site through an auction. All landowners in the region can be required to submit asking prices for their plots and the cheapest offers accepted. Some of the project land will be acquired in the auction itself. Remaining landowners can be given plots purchased around the project site instead of paying them in cash. Determining compensation through a land auction in and around the project site, where the government acquires more land than what is needed for the project, and then allowing farmers to choose between cash and land in a nearby location instead of just cash, stands a much better chance of satisfying farmers. It is also more likely to enable projects that maximize the economic value of land use.[1]

A recent survey of households whose lands were acquired in Singur provides evidence of the heterogeneity of land valuations to owners and the important role this played in opposition to the land acquisition (Ghatak, et al. 2013). The compensation offered by the state government was *on average* equal to the market values reported by the owners. Yet one-third of these owners refused the compensation and opposed the land acquisition. This is partly explained by the inability of compensation offers to include information relevant to market values of individual plots, such as irrigation or multi-cropped status, or proximity to public transport facilities. The survey of acquired households in Singur cited above found this to be a significant cause of under-compensation of owners of multi-cropped plots

---

[1] For details, see Maitreesh Ghatak and Parikshit Ghosh, 2011, 'The Land Acquisition Bill: A Critique and a Proposal', *Economic and Political Weekly of India*, 46(41); a shorter version is Maitreesh Ghatak and Parikshit Ghosh, 2015, 'Empower, Don't Patronise the Farmer', *Indian Express*, 30 March 2015.

relative to market values. These problems would be entirely avoided if compensations were based on bids submitted by owners in auctions.

The auction-based approach can be extended in various directions. The choice of location of a factory can also be decided by extending the auction to a multistage process. At the first stage, the industry in question or government could set a reserve price and minimum quantity of land needed. Different communities can be asked to bid for the factory to be located in their respective regions. These bids can be set equal to the minimum price at which they can in turn procure the necessary amount of land from landowners within their areas (as elicited by a local auction).

The proposed method is designed to kill two birds with one stone. First, it determines a fair price not through government fiat but through a participatory process of competitive bidding where farmers are free to name their own price and choose their form of compensation (cash or land). Second, it fills in for missing or imperfect land markets in the region by reallocating the remaining farmland to those who place the highest economic value on such an asset.

The Indian government has considerable experience with conducting procurement auctions for dealing with private contractors on public projects. Auctions have proved very effective in several countries in recent times, albeit for much more high-tech allocations like spectrum licences. They are also widely employed in procurement of food grain by the Food Corporation of India (FCI) as well as in private wholesale trade. Hence, the administrative expertise needed to conduct auctions for land acquisition is present in abundance. However, decentralizing responsibility to local panchayat bodies in conducting these auctions within their jurisdictions will help minimize the sense of land acquisition being foisted on local communities by state or national governments in a top-down manner. In that case panchayat leaders would have to be trained (or assisted) by bureaucrats to conduct such auctions. But this would help them acquire skills necessary for panchayats to take a more active role in business development within their respective areas.

Had the task been one of acquiring a thousand acres from the vast sea of agricultural land stretching across the country, it would have been cheapest, most efficient and least contentious to do it through an auction. The problem at hand is more restrictive – the acquisition must be a specific thousand acres of contiguous territory. We believe that with only slight modification, essentially the same principles can be applied to this more constrained problem.

Offering alternative forms of compensation

The Singur survey points to the role of income security as an important consideration for deciding to give up land. Ownership of land is associated with farming skills that are non-transferable to other professions. Households exhibited considerable preference for being compensated in alternative ways that incorporate their concern for financial security, time preference and pattern of skills. These concerns exhibited considerable diversity, with a corresponding diversity of preferences over alternative forms of compensation. Hence, a menu of alternative compensation packages and not just lump-sum cash ought to be offered.

In this context, the land pooling scheme that has been attempted in Andhra Pradesh is worth mentioning. It does not offer monetary compensation for land taken, but in exchange for village land taken today, it offers a developed piece of land in the future city. For example, for every fertile acre pooled, the state will return 25 per cent of developed area in the future city. This addresses some of the issues mentioned earlier that make farmers unwilling to give up land and also reduces the incentive to hold out on selling in the hope of benefiting from increasing prices.

Under this scheme, depending on the nature of the land and its use, the possibility of a lump-sum and/or an annual (over a ten-year period) cash compensation is also on the table. There is no need to take the consent of 70 per cent of the total affected families for undertaking a public work on agricultural land, as would be needed for land acquisition, and the terms of transfer can be negotiated with individual landowners.

There are, however, some problems with this scheme. Some farmers regret agreeing to it because cost of living goes up sharply with industrial development and urbanization. Also, there is the risk of the project being delayed or even failing altogether, in which case the land swap aspect of the deal falls through.

Speeding up the Digital India Land Records Modernisation Programme (DILRMP)

The progress of the DILRMP to computerize land records and move towards a system of government-guaranteed titles has been slow and uneven across states. It is important for reducing misallocation in the land market and for improving access to credit. Lessons from initiatives at the state level such as the Bhoomi Project in Karnataka, the 2016 Rajasthan Urban Land (Certification of Titles) Act and the use of blockchain technology to prevent property fraud in Andhra Pradesh should be considered to speed up the process.

Reference

Maitreesh Ghatak, Sandip Mitra, Dilip Mookherjee, and Anusha Nath, 2013, 'Land Acquisition and Compensation in Singur: What Really Happened?', *Economic and Political Weekly of India*, 48(21).

The Solutions

1. Rely on auctions, rather than on bureaucrats making the 'right' choices. If properly designed, auctions will tell you not just how much farmers are actually willing to pay, but also where the best location is for a factory.
2. Each parcel of land is different – some create more revenue than others – so only farmers themselves, through auctions, will be able to put a price on them.
3. There are many other innovative ways to compensate farmers worried about income security – for example, by giving them a share of the finished project or a plot in the township being planned.
4. Digital land records are a must, so that ownership of land can be guaranteed by the government and a real land market can develop.

6

GROWING EXPORTS

The Problems

1. Exports are essential for growth and job creation, as they allow a country to produce for the entire world and not just its own people. But India's exports have underperformed, not only in comparison to the People's Republic of China but also to neighbouring countries like Bangladesh.
2. Many exporters, particularly in industries like textiles that create the most jobs, are small and medium enterprises. These find it particularly hard to fit into global supply chains and get loans. They are also the hardest hit by GST.
3. India's labour force does not have sufficient skills, and labour regulations make it hard for exporters to employ the number of people that would make them more efficient.
4. Our transport infrastructure is insufficient, outdated and badly planned – and bureaucratic red tape makes it even harder for exporters to stay competitive.

India's Exports

Gita Gopinath* and Amartya Lahiri

Summary

Indian export growth has remained tepid. The constraints appear to be generalized: low scale of production, low productivity, institutional frictions. Policy initiatives going forward need to focus on reforms that encourage greater scale, specifically labour reforms that allow easier separation between firms and workers. Specific manufacturing sectors like textiles and electronics can be catalysts for growth and employment if one can encourage scale. Micro policies such as trade agreements, simpler documentation procedures at ports, improved credit access and infrastructural upgrades will help. The ongoing reset of trade relations between the United States and the People's Republic of China may be an opportunity as firms seek alternative trade relationships. Labour-abundant India could be an attractive destination.

---

* Gita Gopinath is Economic Counsellor and Director of Research at the IMF. She contributed to this volume before joining the IMF, when she was John Zwaanstra Professor of International Studies and of Economics at Harvard University. The views expressed in this book are those of the author(s) and do not necessarily represent the views of the IMF, its Executive Board, or IMF management.

Exports are not growing fast enough

In the twenty-five years since 1992, when India began liberalizing its trade regime, India's share of world goods exports rose from 0.5 per cent in 1992 to 1.7 per cent in 2017. The corresponding export share of the much-celebrated Indian service sector rose from 0.5 per cent to 3.4 per cent during the same period. To put these numbers in context, over the same period the Chinese share of world merchandise exports rose from 1.8 per cent to 12.8 per cent. Closer home, Bangladesh more than doubled its share of world merchandise exports in just the last ten years, going from 0.09 per cent in 2007 to 0.2 per cent in 2017. More generally, while the world as a whole exports around 30 per cent of its GDP, the share of exports in India's GDP continues to languish below 20 per cent.

The lethargic pace at which India has increased its exports has constrained its growth, as India has not been able to meaningfully tap external demand for its goods and services. In addition, a tepid export sector has consequences for how productive firms are with their resources. Recent research has shown that firms that engage in exports benefit from increased productivity (Atkin, et al. 2017). Indeed, Indian exporting establishments tend to be more productive than non-exporting establishments.

Relative to world averages, India has a greater share of service exports. While the Indian service sector performance has been very good, it is by no means unique. For example, the somewhat less feted Chinese services sector more than tripled its share of world service exports from 0.9 per cent to 3.8 per cent between 1992 and 2017.

Going forward, however, a combination of rising wage costs and increasing automation of business services may well limit the growth potential of services. In addition, given the relatively low employment generating scope of Indian service sector exports, India has to work towards faster growth of merchandise exports.

The tepidity of merchandise exports does not appear to be related to specific sectoral issues. There are no big non-performers; nor are there examples of stellar performing sectors. Rather, the export landscape seems to mirror the general state of industry in India: a preponderance of small firms operating at low productivity and exhibiting limited growth.

What needs to be done?

A general feature of the Indian production landscape is that Indian firms do not have the domestic environment to compete globally. This can be put down to both macro and micro issues. The macro issues apply to all of manufacturing, with exports being just one sub-sector among many.

Macro issues

- **Scale** is essential for a successful exports sector. Policies that inhibit growth in firm size and productivity inhibit the ability to trade. Hurdles to land acquisition, labour regulations, inadequate power and other infrastructure support, and shortages of skilled labour, all contribute to limiting firm size.
- **Fundamental labour reforms** are needed to encourage large scale, labour-intensive production units, while maintaining

worker rights. This will help traditional export sectors such as textiles as well as others like leatherworks, footwear and wood products. In addition, labour reforms have to be integrated with a more broad-based effort to better manage India's human resources and skills.

- **Better transportation infrastructure:** The government needs to work on improving the integration of different modes of transportation with each other, introducing modern warehousing, streamlining customs formalities and improving integration with logistics and industrial parks. The current state of India's transport infrastructure renders its exporters uncompetitive on the world market; according to a recent World Bank (2018) study, 'firms report that while it takes 11 days for a container to travel from Shanghai to Mumbai, it takes 20 days for it to travel from Mumbai to Delhi'.

Micro issues

- **Improve credit access:** Credit flows to exporters have to be encouraged to grow in order to facilitate exports. The majority of India's exporters are SMEs with limited access to external financing. Bank credit is often their only source of financing. These flows must be stable, so that SMEs can plan their production properly.
- **Simplify the GST:** GST export refunds to SMEs must be expedited to help exports. Refunds are still slow. This means that SMEs are typically under pressure because they may not have enough working capital. SME exports, which are labour-intensive and constitute 40 per cent of total exports, have significantly underperformed recently.

- **Sign a trade agreement with the European Union (EU):** Some of India's major exports such as apparel were excluded from the EU's Generalised System of Preferences (GSP) while countries like Bangladesh benefited from it (over 50 per cent of Bangladesh exports are to the EU). We need to undo this disadvantage. Negotiations with the EU on a preferential trade agreement (PTA) have been ongoing since 2007. An agreement needs to be signed. India's export competitors such as Vietnam have also recently concluded a PTA with the EU.

- **Increase South Asian trade:** South Asia is the world's least economically integrated region. Intra-regional trade accounts for less than 5 per cent of India's total trade.

- **Tariff:** Resist temptations to raise tariff rates in response to temporary economic pressures such as a sudden increase in imports. As most exporters use imported inputs, tariffs reduce the competitiveness of Indian exporters. The tariff reductions from 70 per cent in 1992 to the current 10 per cent level have helped strengthen the economy. Importantly, India has also brought down average tariff rates on intermediate goods to the same level. In fact the only intermediate goods tariffs that remain somewhat high are on food and beverages, where they average 40 per cent. The temptation to reverse the tariff reductions has to be resisted.

In the next two points we raise industry-specific issues that need to be addressed to harness the potential of global supply chains for India's growth. In this we focus on two industries that have particular potential.

- **Globally integrate the electronics industry:** This industry has one of the fastest growing global supply chains, albeit one that India has not been able to benefit from – unlike countries like China, Indonesia and Taiwan. According to the World Bank report quoted above, India's entry into global supply chains faces several major hurdles: (i) poor transport infrastructure, as discussed earlier; (ii) low skill levels of the labour force, which requires firms to make a significant investment in training their workers; (iii) complexity of land acquisition, which makes clustering of upstream and downstream firms difficult;[1] (iv) the overall regulatory environment, which further increases costs; and (v) lengthy and unpredictable import clearance procedures.

- **Revitalize the textiles industry:** This industry has ceded ground to countries like Bangladesh, Sri Lanka and Vietnam over the last decade. The issues are familiar: (i) a preponderance of small-scale establishments; (ii) most units use old (sometimes obsolete) machinery operating with outdated technology; (iii) shortages of semi-skilled labour with sufficient training to run modern machines and production lines; (iv) chronic power shortages, which lead firms to use less productive manual machines; (v) land acquisition problems; and (vi) onerous clearance requirements that impede the inflow of imported inputs and export of processed goods in quick time, which is antithetical to international expectations of just-in-time delivery.

---

[1] See Maitreesh Ghatak's note on land reforms in this volume.

References

David Atkin, Amit Khandelwal, and Adam Osman, 2017, 'Exporting and Firm Performance: Evidence from a Randomized Experiment', *Quarterly Journal of Economics*, 132(2).

World Bank, 2018, *India – Systematic Country Diagnostic: Realizing the Promise of Prosperity*, Washington, DC: World Bank Group, http://documents.worldbank.org/curated/en/629571528745663168/India-Systematic-country-diagnostic-realizing-the-promise-of-prosperity

The Solutions

1. The government will have to make sure that the macroeconomic environment is favourable for trade – by signing trade agreements and by avoiding arbitrary taxes, restrictions and tariffs.
2. Focus on ensuring that SMEs get access to loans, and reform the GST to ensure that it no longer hurts them.
3. Conduct labour reforms together with a comprehensive attempt to raise the Indian workforce's skills.
4. Upgrade the country's transport infrastructure and cut red tape so that Indian producers can get goods to its own markets at least as quickly as China's do.

7

FARMS AND FARMERS

The Problems

1. Too many of India's workers are still engaged in agriculture – and, altogether, they make too little money. Agricultural productivity has to improve if farmers are to earn a decent livelihood.

2. In some parts of India irrigation is yet to reach the farmer; in other parts, tube wells and water-intensive crops have depleted the water table and are causing an environmental crisis.

3. Farmers get too small a share of the eventual price of what they produce – too much is swallowed up by middlemen. Also, they cannot access international or even nationwide markets easily.

4. Food prices are no longer increasing as fast as they used to – but that means farmers' incomes are stagnating, since higher prices meant that they earned more. This is increasing rural distress. Any government would be under political pressure to respond – but how?

Agricultural Reforms

Neelkanth Mishra

The importance of agriculture

As far back as 1880, the first Indian Famine Commission had observed that India had too many people cultivating too little land. And yet, the census shows that workers in agriculture increased from 100 million in 1951 to 260 million in 2011 (Mishra 2017). Recent employment surveys show a drop in the numbers, but more than 40 per cent of India's workforce is still deployed in agriculture – and generate only a sixth of the national income. No economic reform agenda can be complete without addressing agriculture: it may create more impact than most social welfare schemes on improving the lives of the poor.

The 'paradox of plenty'

The problem has become much more acute in recent years due to the paradox of plenty (Mishra 2016). Food demand cannot grow rapidly, particularly given that population growth is decelerating and that Indians want to consume fewer calories per head as their lifestyles change.

Alongside this, however, a substantial improvement in rural infrastructure (roads, phones, electricity) is driving rapid output growth. Supply is outpacing demand, and so India now has surpluses in most food categories. As surpluses bring down food price inflation, a large channel of income transfer from the (mostly rich) food consumers to the (mostly poor) food producers has stalled. Till recently, this food price inflation channel moderated the effect of slow agricultural growth. Since 1960, annualized real growth in agricultural GDP has been just 2.5 per cent, when the agricultural workforce grew 1.6 per cent. But prices growing at 7.5 per cent, and annual nominal income growth of 10 per cent prevented extreme stresses.

Complicating matters further, despite this surplus of food, India continues to suffer from very high, and indeed embarrassing, levels of malnutrition and stunting in children, implying that several categories are still scarce or not cheap enough. Government policies have been too focused on cereals.

Options: Government policies are still geared towards increasing the volume of output – specifically of cereals, which are only about a fifth of total agricultural production. This policy priority is a legacy of the era in which India sought self-sufficiency in food. To cope with the new challenges the government must now focus on encouraging value-addition, crop substitution, exports and disintermediation to ensure that farmers' incomes get the much-needed boost. Agriculture being a state subject, the Central government must creatively use incentives to change/influence state-level policies.

Agricultural Reforms

No.	Suggestion	Type*	Description/Explanation
Immediate action			
1.	Target monopolies in the supply chain	Markets	Improving the farmer's share in the supply chain would be difficult without removing monopolies. The Essential Commodities Act and Agricultural Produce Market Committees (APMCs) allow for the formation of monopolies and cartels that make super-normal profits and correspondingly reduce farmers' revenues. So far the political will to reform these, so that monopolies are broken up, has been lacking.
2.	Direct benefits transfer to supplement income; transition to DBT in fertilizers, linkage to soil health cards (SHCs)	Inputs	Given its enormous scope and unprecedented scale, the recently launched income trasfer scheme should be calibrated on breadth (how many beneficiaries), depth (how much) and frequency (would monthly transfers be better?). Over time, key subsidies must be rolled into it: the transition to Aadhaar-authenticated sales of subsidized fertilizers has moved rapidly, e.g. Linking to SHCs is also important in weeding out large buyers. While subsidies are distortionary, simply directing them well initially is an important first step.

No.	Suggestion	Type*	Description/Explanation
3.	Improvements to the Pradhan Mantri Fasal Bima Yojana	Inputs	Insurance cover is well short of the target, 50 per cent of farmers, in 2018–19. A team of experts at the Centre can work with states continuously to track and re-negotiate premium rates which sometimes reach 40 per cent for some crops. The premium subsidy should be paid in time. Technology use (satellites, drones) is picking up, but can go up significantly higher.

Medium- or long-term changes

No.	Suggestion	Type*	Description/Explanation
4.	Standardize mandi-level infrastructure	Markets	To get a national agricultural market going, standard assaying, sorting and grading facilities are vital. This would also help in implementing price-difference schemes that are necessary to ensure that all small farmers can access the minimum support prices that governments set.
5.	Limit commissions/fees	Markets	These should not exceed 2 per cent of the value of produce.
6.	Expand electronic national agricultural market (e-NAM)	Markets	e-NAM volumes are only 2 per cent of India's total agricultural output. Once processes and fees are standardized and APMC monopolies are unwound, e-NAM must be expanded so that farmers can access the best prices for their produce nationwide. A dispute resolution mechanism is also necessary to protect buyers.

No.	Suggestion	Type*	Description/Explanation
7.	Experiment with income transfers to farmers	Inputs	The Rythu Bandhu (RB) scheme of Telangana should provide data that can help fine-tune such transfers. RB-type schemes need reliable land records, but only a few states have them (see Maitreesh Ghatak's note on land reforms in this volume). It is crucial that transfers not distort acreage allocation choices by farmers.
8.	Increase formalization of tenancy	Inputs	The model tenancy act must be legislated (with amendments). The current system, in which tenant farmers have no formal connection to the land they till, creates inefficiencies in government policy, artificially separating landowners from tenant farmers and small-scale farmers.
9.	Encourage agricultural exports	Markets	Surplus agricultural production must be exported to maximize farmer income. For this the government needs to develop specialist clusters that have processing facilities modern enough to meet export norms (as well as the strict regulations required by many export markets). Trade policy should be stable and predictable, with no sudden tariffs or restrictions. Agriculture being a heavily protected sector globally (Swiss subsidy is 90 per cent of their agri-GDP), trade negotiations can have a big impact on Indian agri-exports.

No.	Suggestion	Type*	Description/Explanation
10.	Encourage crop substitution	Water	The production mix needs to change. First, more of the agri-products demanded by export markets need to be in the mix. Second, the cultivation of water-guzzling crops like sugar cane and rice needs to move from increasingly dry Maharashtra and Punjab to water-surplus states.
11.	Improve technology adoption	Inputs	The adoption of GM cotton dramatically raised production. But since then controversies have prevented progress: a clear policy on GM trials and adoption is necessary. Not just to improve output, but also for needs like bio-fortified foods that can augment nutritional security.
12.	Agricultural research & education	Inputs	India's agricultural research has seen some notable successes, but requires significant expansion in scale and in providing these inputs to farmers. Outreach must be a priority.
13.	Intellectual property rights (IPR) regime	Inputs	Instead of an ad hoc issue-by-issue approach, which is costly, controversial and tends to be erratic, there should be a clear policy that helps Indian farmers access the best technologies at affordable prices.

No.	Suggestion	Type*	Description/Explanation
14.	Address gaps in public irrigation system	Water	Large irrigation schemes with canals are costly, time-consuming, prone to corruption and harder to maintain. Water pipelines can reduce evaporation/leakage and are also faster to put into place.

* Markets = agricultural marketing policies and facilities; Inputs = inputs, including investing in agricultural R&D; Water = water

References

Neelkanth Mishra, 2016, 'Paradox of Plenty', *Indian Express*, 22 August 2016.

Neelkanth Mishra, 2017, 'Beyond the Farm', *Indian Express*, 30 March 2017.

The Solutions

1. The government will have to open up markets for farmers. Cartels, middlemen and monopolies at local wholesale markets will have to be broken up through legal reforms; a national market for agri-produce will have to be created; and agri-exports will have to be prioritized.
2. Water must be a focus of the long-term strategy. Crops that require a lot of water, such as paddy, must shift from semi-desert regions to those which have excess water. Meanwhile, irrigation projects can be speeded up by focusing on water pipelines instead of grandiose canals.
3. Various forms of cash payments to farmers will need technological intervention to work – whether fertilizer subsidies, or a minimum income guarantee, or quicker insurance payouts.
4. Farming must move up the technology ladder; the government must set out a clear and progressive policy on GM crops and on IPR for such things as new seeds.

8

REFORMING ENERGY

The Problems

1. India has become increasingly dependent on imported energy to fuel its growth. This means the health of the economy is very sensitive to global conditions – for example, the price of crude oil. This creates uncertainty and is a drag on growth.
2. India needs to pay for expensive energy imports either through exports or through capital flows into the economy. But capital flows and energy prices often move in different directions, making it hard to ensure these payments are made.
3. As India develops, its energy mix moves from less dense fuel such as firewood to denser fuel like crude oil. Again, this increases external dependency.
4. Power generation has its own problems, with several power plants in danger of being closed down for financial reasons and many state electricity boards chronically unable to avoid losses, because of the political difficulty of raising electricity prices.

Energy Reforms

Neelkanth Mishra

India's energy needs are heavily dependent on imports. This puts downward pressure on growth – it creates undesired volatility in external balances and on medium-term growth expectations.

Productivity is intricately tied to energy usage: not only does more output per capita require greater automation in transportation, industrial output and household chores, it also requires a shift to more energy-intensive materials like metals, plastics, bricks and cement. Growing GDP without growing energy consumption is possible – but it is difficult and has limits. Productivity improvement also needs greater usage of denser fuels (like crude oil and coal) and a decline in the use of less dense biomass (firewood, crop residue). Viewed from another perspective, urbanization, whether in situ or via migration, increases energy demand and needs denser fuels, pushing residential demand towards electricity and gas.

If India sustains the 7 per cent a year growth rate that it has managed on average over the last twenty-five years, and also manages to reduce energy intensity of GDP growth at

2.5 per cent a year as it has since 1995, energy demand would grow at 4.4 per cent a year. However, energy production grew at only 3.1 per cent a year between 2000 and 2015, and so imports had to rise at 8.4 per cent to meet demand.

Import dependency of energy rose from 21 per cent in 2000 to 36 per cent in 2015 and could rise to nearly 50 per cent by 2040 even if energy production rises at a slightly faster pace than it has in the past. Worryingly, with India lacking reserves of the fuel types that are likely to see demand growth, i.e., oil, gas and metallurgical coal, increasing domestic production alone would not suffice.

While energy prices are notoriously volatile, their compounded annual growth rate over a twenty-five-year horizon has rarely been less than 2 per cent: by this yardstick, India's energy import bill could rise to $660 billion by 2040. As a share of GDP this would be lower than it is currently, but it would still pose a challenge: energy imports need to be paid for, either through exports or by getting foreign capital. The rhythm of capital flows being mostly different from that of energy prices, this causes undesirable swings in India's medium-term growth expectations.

Options: The solutions can only lie in a rapid increase of domestic energy **production**, improving energy **efficiency** and encouraging **substitution** to locally produced energy sources. A high energy import bill means that there is pressure on the rupee to lose value; as it depreciates, domestic energy sources become cheaper. So there should be a natural preference for domestic energy. However, government policy needs to accelerate this transition.

Energy Reforms

No.	Suggestion	Type*	Description/Explanation
1.	A mass campaign to generate awareness of the need for energy reforms to sustain high growth	Substitution	Will help build political consensus around SEB reforms (a state subject), energy substitution related projects and improvement of energy efficiency.
Immediate action			
2.	Auction licences for merchant-mining of coal	Production	Enabling legislation already exists for private sector participation in mining. This would help make supply responsive to the price of energy in rupees.
3.	Reintroduce the clean energy cess and deploy it to incentivize SEBs away from coal	Production	The earlier cess of Rs 400/t was subsumed under GST. The new cess can be an add-on, but to be utilized only for energy-related uses (so net neutral for users).
4.	Free up gas pricing	Production	Again, this will help make supply responsive to the energy price in rupees. It will also encourage prospecting for domestic gas resources.
5.	Accelerate retirement of old thermal power plants	Efficiency	While significant energy is wasted in converting coal to electricity, this is particularly bad in older plants.
6.	Reduce non-transport use of diesel	Substitution	Nearly a sixth of diesel is used for purposes other than for transport – e.g., for backup power via gensets. Transitioning to solar

No.	Suggestion	Type*	Description/Explanation
			pump sets and giving incentives to states to reduce planned power outages would help reduce the need for gensets.
7.	Start time-of-day pricing programmes	Production	Start charging bigger customers a different tariff depending on the time of day that they consume power, and extend this over time to everyone. This will enable quicker renewable integration.
8.	Start a procurement programme for renewable power with storage	Production	To have a greater share of renewable generation on the grid one needs grid-scale storage. A government procurement programme can create a supply chain and drive down costs for it.
9.	Electric vehicles (EVs) for taxis, buses, two-wheelers	Substitution	The economics of battery EVs mean these automotive segments are likely to transition first to EVs. Waiting for serendipity to accelerate this transition is risky. Instead, it is better to impose fleet-level carbon emission targets for car makers; continue experimentation with city-specific EV taxis; create incentives for state transport corporations to transition to EV buses.

No.	Suggestion	Type*	Description/Explanation
10.	Revive stranded power plants	Production	For a variety of reasons a significant part of constructed capacity is currently inactive, and is under threat of getting liquidated. Policy must prevent that.

Medium- or long-term changes

No.	Suggestion	Type*	Description/Explanation
11.	Further indigenize renewable energy capacity	Production	Creating a significant amount of solar capacity while there is minimal domestic manufacturing of solar cells would cause the import bill to shoot up and stress external balances. Thus domestic capacity for solar cell production must be created.
12.	Changes to the national power grid	Production	A higher share of renewables in electricity generation would require structural changes to be made to the grid: more storage, different pricing algorithms for power purchase agreements, more micro-grids.
13.	Restructure the SEBs	Efficiency	Currently, one-fifth of power is lost/not billed/ paid for. SEBs are thus very fragile and each should be unbundled into an infrastructure and a services company. The infra company could get a fixed return on its equity, and the services company could compete for customers.

No.	Suggestion	Type*	Description/Explanation
14.	Steelmaking through locally available thermal coal	Substitution	Development of these technologies should be made possible by India's reserves of high-quality iron ore. Nine per cent of India's energy needs is to make steel.
15.	Global benchmarking for major uses of energy	Efficiency	Like water in Israel, Indian households and industry need to use energy most efficiently. Setting industry-level targets will be an important step forward.
16.	Accelerate transition away from direct biomass usage	Substitution	Ujwala is a great start. With electrification and power availability improving, subsidizing households to move to induction cooktops could be tried.
17.	Trading of carbon credits: allow biomass to be included	Substitution	As rural fuels transition to denser sources, the biomass generated every year in farming needs to be used. This may need subsidies initially.
18.	Reducing plastics usage	Substitution	The non-energy usage of gas and oil, such as in the creation of plastics, should be minimized.
19.	Raise targets for renewable energy generation significantly	Production	Even 650 GW of solar + wind capacity would provide only 4 per cent of India's projected energy needs in 2040.

* P = raising **production**; E = improving **efficiency**; S = driving/ encouraging **substitution** to domestic energy sources

The Solutions

1. Renewable energy production is vital – but that would require not just scaling up targets for the number of solar or wind farms, but creating a domestic ecosystem for solar cell and battery production. Taxis, two- and three-wheelers and buses should be incentivized to shift to electric power.

2. Power distribution needs to be reformed. The monopoly of the SEB needs to be broken up, and the power grid upgraded to deal with more renewable energy production. Micro-grids are a powerful local solution, and variable tariffs depending upon the time of day that power is used should be tried.

3. Both distribution companies and consumers should be encouraged to move away from coal or diesel. Cook-stoves should become electric, diesel gensets should be rendered unnecessary and the clean energy cess on coal should be reintroduced.

4. Recent history has shown the utility of mass campaigns for such things as hygiene, sanitation and giving up the LPG subsidy. A similar campaign should be started to change attitudes towards electricity tariffs, renewable power and energy wastage.

9

DEFICITS AND DEBT

The Problems

1. India's government spends more than it earns. The combined fiscal deficit of the state and the Centre is about 7 per cent of GDP – among the highest of any emerging market.
2. States in particular have overspent in recent years. Their budgeting is sometimes not sufficiently clear and their finance commissions are generally short of capacity.
3. A high fiscal deficit means that the economy is more vulnerable. More government borrowing means that private investment is 'crowded out'. While growth may increase in the short run following a fiscal expansion, it can collapse soon thereafter.
4. The government has made many other promises and guarantees that may require it to spend money in the future – these 'contingent liabilities' are also growing.

Responsible Growth: The Way forward for India

Prachi Mishra

Background

While India fares well and has shown significant progress on several macroeconomic indicators like growth, inflation and the current account, **its fiscal performance remains an outlier among emerging markets (EMs).** As shown in Table 1, the consolidated fiscal deficit (for the Centre and the states combined) has consistently been reported at around 7 per cent for most of this decade, which stands as the second highest across EMs (Brazil, which went through a fiscal crisis, being the highest).

Why is sticking to a path of fiscal prudence important for India (see Mishra, et al. 2018)?

1. **Higher general government deficits in India tend to be associated with higher costs of borrowing for both the Centre and the states, reduced capital inflows and lower private investment** (so-called crowding out).
2. **Fiscal and external vulnerabilities are also closely**

Table 1: Key macroeconomic indicators across emerging markets

	Real GDP growth (% over previous year)		Consumer price inflation (% over previous year)		Current account balance (% of GDP)		Fiscal balance (% of GDP)	
	2012–14	2015–17	2012–14	2015–17	2012–14	2015–17	2012–14	2015–17
India	6.2	7.3	8.6	4.4	-3.2	-1.1	-6.7	-6.9
Brazil	1.8	-2.0	6.0	7.0	-3.4	-1.7	-3.8	-9.0
China	7.7	6.8	2.4	1.7	2.1	2.0	-1.7	-3.6
Indonesia	5.5	5.0	5.6	4.6	-3.0	-1.8	-2.1	-2.6
Russia	2.0	-0.5	6.8	8.7	2.5	3.2	-0.4	-2.5
South Africa	2.2	1.1	5.8	5.4	-5.3	-3.3	-4.3	-4.5
Turkey	6.2	5.4	8.4	8.9	-5.6	-4.3	-1.3	-1.7

related.[1] It is widely accepted that an unsustainable fiscal deficit was the primary cause of the 1991 BoP crisis. The years following the global financial crisis when India did not adhere to the envisaged path of fiscal consolidation were also associated with external instability – leading to the taper tantrum episode of 2013 (see the FRBM Review Committee Report, 2017). Indeed, pressure on the currency tends to be higher during times of worsening fiscal balances, especially when the government balance deviates from targets.

3. **Adverse real effects of large fiscal expansions: What can we learn from past experience?** The two largest episodes of fiscal expansion in India's history were during the financial years 1998–99 and 2009–10.[2] While growth picked up temporarily following both these episodes, it slowed down remarkably thereafter. Therefore, any immediate stimulative effects of large fiscal expansions on economic activity in India appear to be outweighed over time by crowding out, and/or the effect of reduced confidence.

Way forward

1. Implement the recommendations of the FRBM Committee, which entails **reducing India's overall debt to 60 per cent of GDP by 2022–23.** The Centre's debt should be reduced to 40 per cent of GDP, and overall states' debt to 20 per cent of GDP by that year.

---

[1] See the note by Sajjid Chinoy on external imbalances in this volume.

[2] Defined as two successive years of at least a percentage point of GDP's worth of fiscal expansion.

2. The key operational target should be the headline fiscal deficit. As envisaged by the FRBM, the **Centre's fiscal deficit and the overall states' fiscal deficit should each be reduced to 2.5 per cent of GDP by 2022–23.**[3]

3. **Set up an independent fiscal council (FC)** as recommended by the FRBM Review Committee. The FC can serve both an ex-ante role – providing independent forecasts on key macroeconomic variables like real and nominal GDP growth, tax buoyancy and commodity prices – and an ex-post monitoring role. It could also serve as the institution to advise on triggering the escape clause from fiscal requirements and also specify a path of return.

4. **Reining in state finances will need to be prioritized.** The fiscal trajectories of the Centre and the states have diverged, with state finances worsening in recent years. Ultimately it is the consolidated fiscal deficit that matters for the real economy, as well as for the markets. In the event of any fiscal crisis, the sovereign will be accountable for the liabilities of the states as well as the Centre.

5. Therefore, **it is imperative to get a comprehensive handle on, and solution to, the contingent liabilities** of the sovereign as a whole, including pension liabilities (see details below).

6. **Each state should review its state-level FRBM Act** and align it with the recommendations of the FRBM

---

[3] See Pranjul Bhandari's note in this volume, 'The Slow Pace of Infrastructure Buildout', for suggestions on how the composition of the fiscal deficit can be adjusted in a growth-enhancing manner.

Review Committee, which have been accepted by Parliament.

7. **Beef up the capacity of the state finance commissions** so they can dig into the details of finances at the state level and be able to engage fruitfully with the state finance ministries and with the Finance Commission of India.

Contingent liabilities of the sovereign in key areas

We discuss key issues and propose the way forward in the case of liabilities in three key areas. These proposals have already been put forward and discussed at length in the FRBM report. There are other contingent liabilities, e.g., in pensions, which are not discussed here.

In power

- **Address the flow problem:** There should be **no further bank financing of the operating losses of state power utilities.** Instead, state governments should make a firm commitment to underwrite the shortfall in the revenue of distribution companies as equity or an interest-free loan on an annual basis.
- **Increase state utilities' revenue:** Distribution companies and state governments must achieve time-bound targets to earn positive revenue. Compulsory metering, technological upgradation and periodic tariff revision and implementation should be adhered to.
- Notably, raising tariffs is bound to increase the incentives for theft, which will show up as an increase in 'aggregate technical and commercial' losses. Therefore, **separate**

measures to address such losses should be taken by all states. Lessons from the Gujarat experience can be used, for example, crackdown on thefts and unmetered power supply and introduce separate feeder lines for different segments.[4]

- **Cut down the role of intermediaries:** A framework should be developed to facilitate electricity generation companies to directly sell their surplus power to consumers at a negotiated price. Further, open access policies, charges and other non-price barriers at the state level should be revisited so that final consumers can benefit from a wider set of choices and the lowest prices. Producers could also then sell, perhaps across state borders, to the destination with the best price.

In food

- State governments maintain food credit accounts with commercial banks. The credit is used by certain states for centralized procurement of cereals on behalf of the Food Corporation of India. There are long delays in servicing these accounts, particularly in some states. These arise mainly due to disputes between those state governments and the FCI that delay the reimbursement of procurement expenses to the state concerned. These accounts should have long ago been classified as NPAs.
- **Food credit to centralized procurement states should**

---

[4] Kaur and Chakraborty (2018) show how the financial and operational efficiency parameters envisaged in the Ujwal DISCOM Assurance Yojana have not yet been met by many participating states.

be routed only through the FCI, duly guaranteed by the Government of India. This would streamline the process, improve its efficiency and minimize the disputes between procuring states and the FCI that lead to persistent irregularities in the food credit account of the concerned states. A comprehensive special audit of grain stocks should be conducted to accurately determine the level of irregularities that have already built up, and these should be settled by the Central government and the FCI as soon as possible.

In government-sponsored credit guarantee schemes

- The Government of India has launched many credit guarantee schemes – the Credit Guarantee Fund Trust for Micro and Small Enterprises (CGTMSE), Credit Risk Guarantee Fund Scheme for Low Income Housing, and so on – to increase the flow of formal credit to various targeted beneficiaries. These credit guarantee schemes may have helped the intended beneficiaries to get credit at more favourable terms, but **it is important that these schemes are run in a prudent and transparent manner.**
- While the Government of India has made an explicit assurance that it will fund these schemes if their corpus runs short, **it is important to make sure that the schemes are run well so that loan losses are minimized,** and that they are kept adequately funded on an ongoing basis, based on certain prudential norms.

References

FRBM Review Committee Report, 2017, https://dea.gov.in/sites/default/files/Volume 1 FRBM Review Committee Report.pdf

Amandeep Kaur and Lekha Chakraborty, 2018, 'UDAY Power Debt in Retrospect and Prospects: Analyzing the Efficiency Parameters', NIPFP Working Paper No. 244.

Prachi Mishra, Vishal Vaibhaw, and Andrew Tilton, 2018, 'Fiscal Prudence: Pain or Gain for India?', *Asia in Focus*, Goldman Sachs Economic Research.

The Solutions

1. By 2022–23, the Union government's fiscal deficit should be brought down to 2.5 per cent of GDP, as should the states' combined fiscal deficit. This will help private borrowing take off. India's overall debt-to-GDP ratio should come down to 60 per cent.
2. An independent fiscal council should be set up that can monitor the fiscal deficit, project the future path of key macroeconomic indicators and manage the response to emergencies that require more spending.
3. State government deficits will need to be reined in and state finance commissions given more resources. State-level fiscal responsibility legislation will have to be updated.
4. The government should work on clarifying the scope of its 'contingent liabilities', which emerge out of its various promises and guarantees. Action will be needed to clean up pensions, power, food and credit guarantee schemes – any and all of which could cause a major fiscal pile-up in the future.

10

FIXING SCHOOLS

The Problems

1. The quality of education in India is very low. The majority of students who have technically completed primary school are neither literate nor numerate.
2. Within a single school class, students can be of vastly different levels of achievement – and this inequality increases as you move through school. This makes teaching very difficult – and the least accomplished students effectively learn nothing.
3. An emphasis on 'passing exams' has meant that students focus on memorization rather than on picking up useful skills and concepts. Vocational training is not considered important.
4. The Right to Education has expanded access – but at the cost of forcing many private schools to shut down.

Reforming the Indian School Education System*

Karthik Muralidharan

A fundamental source of tension in the design of an education system comes from the fact that, historically, education systems have served two very different purposes.

First, they have sought to impart knowledge, skills and shared concepts of identity and citizenship. We can broadly refer to these as the 'human development' role of education.

However, education systems have also served a second purpose, which is to assess and classify students on the basis of educational ability and achievement and to select higher achieving students for higher education and occupations that aim to attract the most meritorious students. We can refer to this as the 'sorting' function of education.

A quick summary of Indian education history after Independence would suggest that the education system for the most part is driven by sorting rather than human

* These are the author's personal views and reflect inputs provided to the committee writing the New Education Policy for India and to the 'Economic Strategy for India (2018)' put together by a non-partisan group of economists. This version is as of 15 February 2019.

development. Indeed, the Indian education system in its current form is perhaps best understood as a 'filtration' system rather than an 'education system'.

Using this framework helps make sense of several deep structural challenges of the Indian education system that have been widely remarked upon.

1. There are **massive inequalities** in the overall education system – which on the one hand routinely produces students who go on to achieve global excellence in their fields and on the other hand produces the world's largest number of primary-school-completing students who are not functionally literate and numerate at even a second- or third-grade level.

   a. A major reason for this is that the syllabus and textbooks have not changed from a time when a much smaller fraction of students were in the education system. Since the focus of the system continues to be on 'passing' exams linked to the syllabus, children who fall behind the curriculum often end up learning close to nothing despite attending school.[1]

   b. This is because teachers, parents and students are not rewarded for improving learning at levels below the current grade level, because it will not help in passing the grade-level exam – and so students who fall behind early are left behind in perpetuity.

2. An obsessive focus on exams and marks has led to an education system characterized by **rote learning** to pass exams (often through cramming of past exam papers) as opposed to conceptual understanding that can be applied and used in practical situations.

---

[1] As shown in Muralidharan, Singh, and Ganimian (2019).

a. This is also in part a consequence of point (1), because the only viable strategy for students who fall behind is to cram for exams and hope to pass them by having memorized questions that may appear in the exam.

b. Conceptual understanding is not prioritized as it is not rewarded by the exam system.

3. Very **low levels of practical skills** even among students who have notionally 'passed' various exams and possess various levels of paper qualifications.

Note that there is nothing wrong with sorting per se. Every society around the world aims to identify its most talented citizens and match them into leadership roles and occupations that affect society as a whole. It is also completely rational both for institutions of higher learning and employers to seek credible signals about the level of learning in preparation of students and for students to seek to credibly provide the signals.[2]

Further, sorting-based education systems may well have been efficient for agrarian societies where the fraction of knowledge-based jobs was small and where the economic and social returns to education were limited for those in agrarian and manual labour. However, the modern knowledge-based economy requires every citizen to be educated to the point where they are empowered to build their skills and capabilities continuously, and on their own initiative.

---

[2] This is why well-intentioned ideas such as scrapping the tenth board exam are highly counterproductive in practice. Scrapping the signal does not remove the need for one and it ends up disproportionately hurting disadvantaged students who do not have other options for signalling their talent.

However, the problem with the sorting paradigm of education is that children who fall behind (overambitious) grade-level standards do not get a meaningful education because there is no provision for 'teaching at the right level'. This has led to a massive waste of both time and money. Money is spent on building schools and hiring teachers, and effort is focused on keeping children in school (to prevent 'dropout'), but very little actual learning is taking place (see evidence reviewed in Muralidharan [2013] for details).

The central design challenge for the Indian education system is that it was designed for sorting and not for human development. Almost every structural weakness of the Indian education system can be explained by this framework.

Turn to Appendix A for an illustration of the scale of this challenge. Indeed, perhaps the most important graphs to understand school education in India are provided in Appendix A based on data from Delhi and Rajasthan.

Thus, a fundamental goal for Indian education policy has to be to move the education system from a sorting and selection paradigm to a human development paradigm, one that will empower every citizen to be educated enough to have the foundation needed for a lifetime of continuous learning in whichever area of skill he or she may seek to learn.

The core building blocks for achieving this goal include:

1. Curriculum reform to reduce content and emphasize understanding.
2. Exam reform to provide both 'absolute' and 'relative' credentials.

3. A national mission to achieve universal functional literacy and numeracy by grade three.
4. Universal preschool education to support school readiness before grade one.
5. Reform of teacher training to emphasize pedagogy over theory.
6. Having greater clarity on the role of the state and the market in providing education in India – and both leveraging the private sector to achieve India's education goals and regulating it adequately as needed (this requires reforms to the RTE Act).
7. Creating high-quality vocational education streams in school and integrating these with practicum-based training programmes for vocational education (in grades seven to twelve).

It is also essential for the education policy to emphasize certain key cross-cutting themes that have been neglected for the most part in education policy discourse in India – which so far has focused more on 'what' to do rather than on 'how' to do it in a manner that is compatible with fiscal and capacity constraints. These include:

1. Using evidence and research to better inform policy choices.
2. Cost-effectiveness.
3. Governance.

The cross-cutting themes are discussed first, followed by a more elaborate discussion of the seven building blocks identified above:

Themes

1. **Using evidence and research to better inform policy choices:** The last fifteen years have seen a sharp increase in the quality of evidence available on the effectiveness of various policies at improving education outcomes. Yet, this evidence is typically not reflected in the 'business as usual' policy choices that are made by the Union and state governments. Thus, while education policy makers should definitely conduct extensive consultations, it is essential to put more weight on recommendations backed by high-quality evidence.

2. **Cost-effectiveness:** A second key theme is that of cost-effectiveness of policy recommendations. Prior education policy exercises have been strong in articulating visions for education, but have usually paid less attention to the details of **how** this vision can be achieved keeping in consideration the financial and administrative constraints within which policies have to be framed and implemented. Given the combination of fiscal constraints and strong needs for spending in several sectors, a responsible policy exercise has to consider the cost-effectiveness of various policy options to achieve a given set of goals.

   In particular, the evidence from high-quality studies above suggests that it may be possible to achieve sharp improvements in education outcomes even without increasing spending – by reallocating expenditure from less to more cost-effective interventions and policies. Since it is often politically difficult to cut any kind of existing spending, at the very least it is important to allocate new spending for education in cost-effective ways.

It is worth paying special attention to the issue of teacher salaries, which comprise the largest component of education spending. Several studies have shown that there is no correlation between the level of teacher salaries and their effectiveness at improving learning outcomes. Yet, it is likely that many states will implement the Seventh Pay Commission award, which will absorb the major part of any increase in education spending in the coming decade, while being highly unlikely to improve learning outcomes.[3]

Thus, it is essential for the Union government to strongly urge state governments to innovate, evaluate cost-effective options for improving education outcomes, and use the fiscal and policy space provided by the Fourteenth Finance Commission award to try to pivot education expenditure from less to more cost-effective policies.

3. **Governance:** A last cross-cutting theme that is central to achieving the goals of the new education policy is governance. Studies in the past decade have identified shocking weaknesses in the education governance in the country. Thus, India has, for example, high rates of teacher absenteeism, as well as high rates of vacancies in key supervisory positions including block and district

---

[3] A particularly striking example is provided from a high-quality study of unconditional teacher salary increases in Indonesia, where the government doubled teacher pay in 2005 – but this very large increase led to no improvement in student learning (de Ree, et al. 2017).

education officers. These officials are also transferred frequently (their average tenure is less than a year), which makes effective governance very difficult.

Here we recommend that the national education policy follow the guidelines established by the NITI Aayog under its School Education Quality Index initiative.

The goal of the state-level SEQI is to institutionalize a focus on improving education outcomes (learning, access, equity) as the principal aim of school education policy in India. It also recognizes that school education is primarily a state subject and aims to encourage state-level leadership in improving outcomes in cost-effective ways.

It is hoped that the annual calculation and dissemination of the SEQI, with a focus on measuring and highlighting the **annual improvement** of states, will:

a. Shift the policy focus to outcomes rather than inputs and programmes.

b. Encourage state-led innovation in cost-effective policy approaches to improve outcomes.

c. Facilitate documentation and sharing of best practices across states.

The SEQI has developed a series of governance indicators that states will be measured and ranked on, and against which progress will be tracked over time. These indicators reflect a high-level consensus on key governance indicators, and we urge the Ministry of Human Resource Development and the NITI Aayog to monitor progress on these.

We now turn to discussing the substantive topics.

1. **Curriculum reform to reduce content and emphasize understanding:** There is already a lot of good content and ideas in the Yash Pal Committee report on the New Curricular Framework that has not been acted on. So this section will be brief.

   The current curriculum has way too much content, which in turn pushes the education system to deliver rote learning as opposed to conceptual understanding. A content-heavy approach is again consistent with a sorting system since the sheer volume of material to be covered makes it more likely that students with better natural academic aptitude (as opposed to better 'educated' students) will score better on exams.[4]

   In an age when factual information is easily available on the Internet (which in turn is increasingly widely available through smartphones), the premium on memorization and regurgitation of facts is falling sharply relative to the ability to be able to ask and answer relevant questions by finding facts and opinions from different sources, assessing their relative merit and being able to effectively synthesize such content for better understanding and decision-making.

---

[4] For instance, exams for selecting bureaucrats in ancient China required the memorizing of extensive amounts of Confucian text. Mastery of these texts would have likely provided only limited training in 'how' to be a better administrator, but the sheer volume of content ensured that only students of naturally higher ability were likely to pass the exam. This is a classic example of a sorting-based system as opposed to a human development one.

Thus, a core goal of education policy should be to simplify and narrow down the volume of topics covered and emphasize instead the ability to understand concepts, connect concepts across topics and apply them creatively in solving newer problems.[5]

2. **Exam reform to provide both 'absolute' and 'relative' credentials:** It is important for education reformers to recognize that despite the best intentions of educationists and national leaders to have education systems reflect a broader set of goals, the single most important determinant of what teachers, parents and students work towards is the content and structure of the exam system. Indeed, the examination system is the proverbial tail that wags the dog of the entire education system.

Thus, reorienting the education system towards a human development paradigm as opposed to a sorting paradigm will require a fundamental rethinking of the examination system in India, which in its present form is almost completely oriented towards the sorting function. As explained above, it is not viable in practice to wish away the sorting function of an education system. The problem with the status quo, however, is that:

a. Improvements in learning that are at levels significantly below the examination threshold are completely undervalued by all stakeholders (parents, students

---

[5] For secondary and higher secondary school, a related concept is to try to follow the US system a bit in terms of 'modularizing' the content of maths and science syllabi in high school. A certain amount of tracking is then made feasible, with students working their way through 'modules' at a variable pace as opposed to the entire class following the same textbook and syllabus with no differentiation.

    and teachers) because such improvements will not
    be seen in the current exam system.[6]

b. Thus, the default of instruction in the classroom pretty
    much follows the textbook and syllabus – regardless
    of the fact that the vast majority of students (at least
    in government schools) are way behind the curricular
    standards of the syllabus (see Appendix A).

c. As a result, students who fall behind grade-level
    standards before completing eighth grade typically
    learn very little in class. Their only hope of managing
    with the expectations of school is to attend coaching
    classes, cram from past test papers and hope to
    somehow pass exams (typically with very little
    understanding of the content).

d. While the labour market cares about actual skills,
    there is no credible way of learning about a student's
    'absolute' level of understanding/mastery of a concept.
    This is because the marks on a grade-level exam
    mainly serve to 'rank' students for admission to higher
    levels of education and do not convey any information

---

[6] A great example of this is provided from a recent study in Delhi of the
effectiveness of an after-school computer-aided learning programme
(Muralidharan, Singh, and Ganimian 2019). The programme was
incredibly effective in improving learning outcomes of upper primary
students in grades six to nine targeted by the programme (way more
effective in a faster time than any other intervention evaluated with
comparable rigour in India). However, these learning improvements
were taking place at a level of learning that was two or three grade levels
below the currently enrolled grade. Thus, the substantial improvements
in learning were *not* seen on the grade-appropriate school exam. This
may explain why parental demand for the programme was low even
though it was so effective at improving learning.

to parents, students or employers about the absolute level of mastery of any relevant skills.

Thus, part of key reforms must be a national testing agency that can prescribe standards for 'absolute' levels of proficiency at topics, which are broken down at a much more granular level by subject and grade (similar to how software-based learning applications like Khan Academy and Mindspark are structured).

The availability of modular assessments that are organized in ascending order of skills will provide a critical source of feedback to parents, teachers, students and employers about the absolute competence that a student has attained and about the progress made at regular intervals (say, every month to three months).

While exams will continue to serve a sorting function based on student rank, the goal is for the education system to focus on absolute progress made by each student relative to his/her own prior level (regardless of the rank of the student in class and the extent to which he/she is behind the grade-level standards).

Thus, the nature of assessments will need to shift from saying 'Student X scored Y per cent in the class five exam' to saying 'Student X has demonstrated the following levels of absolute competence in various topics/ domains'. The levels can range from 'not demonstrated' to 'mastered' and would aim to provide feedback to parents and students (and eventually employers) about functional competencies as opposed to arbitrary marks.

In the long term, such assessments can be administered through technology-based platforms – which would enable dynamic adaptive tests and also ensure integrity of measurement through large item banks. But, in the short term, such assessments can be carried out through pre-printed worksheets for various topics.

This is an incredibly important reform to ensure that the millions of children who are behind grade level and at risk of being left behind permanently are encouraged to make 'absolute' progress regardless of their level. It is also a critical enabler of skilling and vocational education for students who may not take an academic track.

A key challenge for the skilling sector in India today is that the students who enter skilling or job-training programmes have very poor literacy and numeracy – and are thus often not equipped even to handle the curriculum of the skilling programmes. This is because by the time students are earmarked for vocational tracks in school and directed to such programmes, they have already fallen far behind the curriculum and have weak foundational skills.

Having credible signals of absolute credentials of learning will help students, parents, teachers, providers of higher education (including vocational and skill-based education), as well as employers.

3. **A national mission to achieve universal functional literacy and numeracy:** The single biggest failing of the Indian education system is the fact that seventy years after Independence, the majority of children completing primary education are still not functionally literate and numerate. This is both an economic and a moral failure. The lack of such foundational literacy and numeracy both inhibits the skill formation needed for economic

growth and also robs millions of children and youth of the opportunity to participate in the broader economic growth of the country – and to become empowered citizens who are able to navigate a fast-changing world.

We believe therefore that the **single most important outcome that education policy needs to deliver on for the future of the country is to ensure, by 2022, universal functional literacy and numeracy of all schoolchildren by the end of grade three.** Indeed, the history of Indian education policy suggests that trying to do too much may have prevented it from achieving even the basics.

Thus, even if the entire education system is able to achieve just this one goal in the next few years in mission mode and establish processes to make sure that every cohort entering school starting in the academic year 2019–20 has achieved universal functional literacy and numeracy by the end of third grade, that will be an enormous success.

Achieving this goal will be enabled by three key sets of investments. The first is **universal preschool education** to ensure better school readiness by the start of first grade (described in further detail below). The second is providing **supplemental instructional support to children who are falling behind** in the early grades itself to ensure that every child is functionally literate and numerate by the end of grade three (this is especially important for the children currently in school). The third is **investing in independent measurement and monitoring** of the achievement of these goals (at least at the district level) and motivating the entire district education machinery to achieve these goals through a suitable combination of recognition and rewards.

The most essential immediate (and easily actionable) step to enable this is supplemental instructional support in the early grades. This support will be for small-group instruction that is pitched appropriately at the level of the student. Consultations with teachers clearly indicate that they are aware of this need – but are not able to simultaneously complete the curriculum in the textbook while also providing such supplemental instruction for children falling behind. At the same time, a large body of high-quality evidence (based on randomized controlled trials) from multiple states in India has shown that it is possible to achieve rapid progress in foundational literacy and numeracy within a few months provided children are taught in small groups at the right level – even if this instruction is delivered by modestly educated (secondary or higher secondary school level) youth from the same area (Banerjee, et al. 2007; Banerjee, et al. 2017).

We therefore recommend a budget be provided to every school for the hiring of part-time tutors (who could even be students in secondary or higher secondary school from the same village/area) to be able to provide such supplemental instruction. Such tutors can work under the guidance of regular teachers and provide one to two hours of supplemental instruction every day to students grouped by their learning level. Combined with independent monitoring of learning outcomes, such an approach is likely to be successful in a cost-effective way.

Note that we do *not* recommend the return to a para-teacher or 'shiksha karmi' model (which has weaknesses on multiple fronts including professional, legal and political). Rather, the extra budget to hire part-time tutors can be seen as a way of supporting a five-year national mission to ensure universal foundational literacy in numeracy.

In the medium to long term, as part of a systematic reform of teacher training and preparation, we recommend a new approach to pre-service teacher training that emphasizes substantial amounts of practical teaching as part of the training/credentialing process (see details below). Over time, we recommend that the time spent in such practical training by students training to become teachers can be focused on providing the small-group supplemental instruction needed to achieve this goal.

4. **Universal preschool education to support school readiness before first grade:** Large gaps in learning levels emerge even in the early years of schooling, attributable in large part to the substantial increase in first-generation learners in the schooling system. Thus we strongly recommend a national commitment towards universal preschool education to support school readiness and help achieve the goal of universal functional literacy and numeracy by grade three.

In practice, there are two different approaches to implementing this goal. The first is to add a year of kindergarten to the school education system. The second is to strengthen the quality of early childhood education in the anganwadi centres, by adding an extra anganwadi worker who is dedicated to delivering early childhood education (which will allow the current worker to continue focusing on child nutrition and health). There are advantages and disadvantages to both approaches, as outlined below.

The main advantages of the anganwadi-based model include:

a. Greater proximity to households (this is important because attendance is highly sensitive to distance at younger ages).

b. The curricular needs of early childhood education are substantially different from those of school education and need to focus more on play, self-regulation, social skills and school readiness more generally. This may require specific forms of training and may be better delivered in an anganwadi centre. There is a risk that preschool education that is based in schools may simply result in standard classroom instruction being conducted at a younger age (since such a structure is likely to draw on teachers who are currently teaching primary grades).

c. Since anganwadi workers are typically hired locally in the same village, they are both more connected to the local communities and likely to have lower rates of absenteeism (compared to teachers who typically live in urban areas and commute to rural postings).

d. Finally, the anganwadi-worker-based model is likely to be much more cost-effective (even after adding an extra anganwadi worker to each anganwadi centre to focus on early childhood education) than a model based on hiring more regular teachers in government schools. Given the fiscal constraints in expanding early childhood education, this is a very important consideration and is likely to make it easier to scale across the country.

i.   For instance, based on recent research in Tamil Nadu on the impact of adding an extra worker to anganwadis to focus on early childhood education, we estimate that the present discounted value of the policy was Rs 16,000–20,000 per month. Thus, the investment in the extra worker would be cost-effective at a monthly salary under this range but not above.

ii. At present costs, it would be cost-effective to add an anganwadi worker to focus on early childhood education (since average monthly anganwadi worker salaries range from Rs 4000–10,000). But given regular teacher salaries of Rs 30,000–60,000, the school-based model would not be cost-effective.

However, the primary-school-based model too has some advantages. These include:

a. Greater ease of attendance for siblings when the older child is of schoolgoing age, while the younger child is of preschool age.

b. Greater scale in terms of facilities.

c. Potentially doable at lower cost if the system has a large number of 'surplus' teachers due to declining enrolment in government schools (but this should likely not be a reason to expand regular teacher hiring).

d. Finally, the quality of the anganwadi system varies widely across states and it is possible that the anganwadi system in some states is too dysfunctional to rely on for early childhood education.

Thus, while the factors above point towards the likely superiority of the anganwadi-based model, it is important to recognize the variation across states and not impose a specific model – as long as states deliver on universal early childhood education.

5. **Reform of teacher training to emphasize pedagogy over theory and the inclusion of extensive practical training. Pre-service training:** The teacher is the single most important determinant of the quality of education received by the student, and it is hoped that having qualified/credentialed teachers will help improve the quality of education – indeed, a cornerstone of the RTE is a requirement that all teachers possess a formal teacher training credential.

Unfortunately, this requirement is not supported by the evidence. In particular, several studies have shown that **there is no correlation between a teacher possessing a formal teacher training credential and his or her effectiveness in the classroom** as measured by improvements in learning outcomes during the period that students are with that teacher (Kingdon and Teal 2010; Muralidharan and Sundararaman 2011; Muralidharan 2012).

Of course, this does not imply that teacher training cannot be effective. However, the evidence is also very clear that the status quo of teacher training is broken and ineffective (this point is also made clearly in the Justice Verma Commission report of 2012). Two of the several reasons for this are particularly important.

The first is the poor quality of the majority of teacher training institutes, especially the ones based on distance learning or correspondence courses (which have no practical training at all). Second, a content analysis of even the better teacher training programmes indicates that the curriculum mostly emphasizes the history, theory, sociology and philosophy of education and has very little focus on pedagogy and also very little practical training. In contrast, global evidence suggests that the most effective forms of training in professional roles involves extensive practical training and learning on the job (Muralidharan 2016).

We therefore recommend a new paradigm for teacher training and professional development that places much more emphasis on **practical training through apprenticeship** as part of the teacher credentialing process. Specifically, we recommend that the ideal structure for pre-service teacher training should intersperse modules of theory with extensive amounts of practicum-based training that will lead to formal teacher training credentials that reflect this practical experience and learning.

We recommend the setting up of a few apex teacher training institutes in each state (in highly reputable public and non-profit private institutes) to design such a programme. We also recommend that such practicum-based teaching degrees are four years long and admit students after class twelve. For elementary school teachers this would result in a B.El.Ed. (practice) degree and feature at least six months of classroom-based practical training each year so that over a period of four years at least half the time is spent on training in the classroom. For secondary-grade teachers, such a programme could be five years long and combine a three-year bachelor's degree in a subject with a year of education theory and a year of practical training.

We also recommend a close integration of such training programmes with the public schooling system, so that trainees are effectively integrated into the schools where practical training will take place and **can provide meaningful instructional support in these schools**. Consistent with RTE norms, the trainees will not be responsible for classes on their own, but will function under the close guidance and supervision of the regular teachers and assist in instructional tasks (especially small-group instruction to support the achievement of universal functional literacy and numeracy for all primary school students).

During the period of practical training, we expect that the training institution will continue to engage with the students through online and smartphone-based interactions – including viewing videos and answering quizzes, writing reflections of their teaching experience and participating in virtual communities of practice with other trainees. Thus, the goal is to achieve a deep integration between theory and practice and reflection on how the two inform each other during the course of pre-service teacher training.

We expect such a teacher training programme to be both prestigious and coveted since (a) the number of places will be limited and admission will be restricted to top scoring twelfth standard graduates, (b) the fees will be waived/subsidized for many students because the practical training includes an element of serving underserved areas, and (c) students will also get a modest stipend (paid for by the education department) for their months of practical training when they will be working in schools.

To address the challenge of spatial mismatch between where the academically strongest students are (typically urban areas) and where the teaching needs in the government schools are the greatest (typically rural areas), we recommend that admission to such a prestigious integrated teacher training programme be geographically dispersed.

For instance, one approach would be to **admit the highest scoring applicant from each panchayat into the programme**, with the understanding that the practical training will be based in a government school in the same panchayat. A further advantage of such an approach is that it enables greater female participation in rural areas by providing training/employment opportunities in the same village. Various aspects of reservations and quotas can also be implemented but may need to be achieved at the district or block levels.

Over time, we also recommend that the process of hiring regular teachers give extra points for each year of actual teaching experience (with years spent as part of practical training counting for credit). Our vision therefore is that in the long term almost all teachers hired into the regular government teaching positions will have completed such integrated practicum-based teacher training programmes.

Such an approach will have several advantages including:

a. Improving the quality of pre-service teacher training by requiring actual pedagogical experience as part of the credentialing process.

b. Improving the ability of trainee teachers to absorb the significance of the theoretical content that is present in typical programmes by observing how these issues matter in practice.

c. Ensuring that teachers entering the education system with permanent jobs (as is typical for government teachers) would have had adequate experience in classroom management and functioning as teachers before obtaining lifetime appointments.

d. Providing a cost-effective way of augmenting instructional resources in government schools. In particular, this would be a more sustainable way of enabling schools to have the teaching resources to provide small-group supplemental instruction for first-generation learners to ensure universal foundational literacy and numeracy for all future cohorts of children in the Indian education system.

We believe that implementing such an approach to pre-service teacher training can be transformative in improving the long-term quality of Indian education both through its impact on improving the pipeline of entrants into the teaching profession and through its immediate impact on ensuring universal foundational literacy and numeracy (through the supplemental instruction provided by the trainees as part of their practical training).

While this approach can help in improving the long-term quality of teachers, urgent attention is also needed to be given to the problem of in-service training for the hundreds of thousands of incumbent teachers, many of whom have entered the system with very poor pre-service training. The biggest challenge in implementing such in-service training is the complete lack of visibility on the quality of such training. Thus, while most states' teacher policies provide for around twenty days a year of in-service training, in practice these trainings are of extremely variable quality and our interactions with stakeholders suggest that these are typically not effective.

Thus, improving the quality of in-service training needs to focus on a few key principles. First, emphasizing effective pedagogy (especially through sample demonstration lessons to illustrate various aspects of effective pedagogy including content, engagement, inclusion and student support). Second, it needs to curate the quality of the in-service training programmes. Third, it needs to ensure that the training is actually done as per the regulatory norms and that **teachers are assessed on their comprehension of the training content**.

We recommend that the most promising practical way of achieving these goals is to make much more use of online teacher training content. Specifically, we recommend developing a **portal for in-service teacher training** that can host thousands of videos (including translations in all major Indian languages) and training modules for various topics that are relevant for in-service teacher training. For instance, a training module could illustrate how to teach the class in an interactive way that engages students, as opposed to simply reading from the textbook and writing on the blackboard, and demonstrate this with short videos. Others could illustrate effective ways of teaching specific concepts. Yet others could illustrate inclusive teaching practices that engage all students and not just the academically stronger ones.

Such a portal would be able to achieve all the principles outlined above. The modules would emphasize pedagogy and provide the training in modular bits as opposed to day-long programmes (research strongly suggests that students are more likely to absorb new material in capsules rather than traditional lecture-based instruction). The portal would allow teachers to rate the quality and usefulness of different kinds of content and therefore create a crowdsourced way of identifying high-quality content (which would reflect the wisdom of teachers around the country). Finally, by providing each teacher with a unique ID to access the portal, it becomes easy to track usage, absorption of materials (through short quizzes at the end of modules) and completion of annual in-service training targets. Over time, modules can be organized into courses, and demonstrated mastery of the content of in-service training courses can become an input into identifying effective teachers and promoting them into roles of greater leadership and responsibility.

The Diksha portal developed by the Ministry of Human Resource Development implements these principles for content creation, but delivering full potential will also depend on integration into teacher evaluations, increments and promotions along the lines outlined above.

6. **Private school regulation and RTE reforms:** While Central and state departments of government mostly focus on government-run schools (for which they have implementation responsibility), **it is imperative that education policy accounts for the large prevalence of private school providers.** Recent estimates suggest that over 40 per cent of school enrolment in India is in private schools, with the share being over 70 per cent in several large cities (FICCI and Ernst & Young Report 2014). The total share of private school enrolment in the twenty largest states is around 55 per cent at the secondary and higher secondary levels.

A national education policy should focus on the quality of education received by every student in India and not distinguish between a student enrolled in a public or in a private school. Thus, a critical enabler of improving education quality in India is expanding the supply of high-quality institutions (both public and private).

However, there are severe constraints on the entry of high-quality private school providers – most notably placed by the RTE. We now have data to assess the implementation of the RTE to offer an informed view on how this has affected education quality and availability in India.

There are two important reforms to RTE provisions on private schools that we recommend:

a. **Regulation of private schools based on disclosure and not based on input mandates:** The RTE's input-based approach to education quality never made sense given the extensive evidence that most school inputs are neither necessary nor sufficient for improving learning outcomes. This has led to an unnecessary and disruptive closure of several low-cost private schools that parents were choosing of their own accord. In many cases, even government schools are in violation of these input-based norms. We therefore recommend:

Repealing all input-based mandates for schools under the RTE (for both public and private schools) and changing the approach to regulation of private schools **to be based on transparency and disclosure as opposed to input-based mandates.** By focusing regulation on disclosure, policy would acknowledge the considerable variation across India and allow diversity of models of effective schooling to emerge. Regulation is still important, and private schools can and should still be sanctioned for lying, but they should not have to meet input mandates.

Such an approach will facilitate (as opposed to inhibit) the expansion of quality private-school providers and allow for variation in approaches across locations and providers. As an aside, it would also facilitate localized cost-effective innovations by government schools, which may be made difficult by the RTE (such as hiring tutors without formal teaching credentials for providing supplemental instructional support).

b. **Introduce a national policy for charter schools (that will at least permit serious pilots):** The goal of RTE Clause 12c was to provide students from economically weaker sections (EWS) the opportunity to attend private schools, and it aimed to reimburse private schools for this.

The fundamental problem with this approach is that it was **based on confiscating existing capacity in private schools for a social purpose as opposed to creating new capacity.** Further, it was deeply illiberal in that it was basically a stealth nationalization of a quarter of private schooling capacity without adequate compensation. Finally, data over the past five years show that several states have (a) set the reimbursement rates considerably below the norms in the law, and (b) in many cases not reimbursed private schools in a timely manner.

The consequence has been a steady shutting down of non-minority private schools that have not been able to bear the burden of the cross-subsidy imposed on them by the RTE.

We therefore propose that RTE Clause 12c be replaced with an approach to public–private partnerships that achieves the equity aims of RTE Clause 12c while also increasing the supply of high-quality education options in India.

Specifically, global evidence suggests that charter schools – **which are public schools that do not charge fees** (because they receive public funding equal to the per-child variable cost in the public system) **and cannot admit students selectively**, but managed by private entities with operational autonomy (especially over teacher hiring and accountability) – have been successful at substantially improving outcomes for disadvantaged students while also increasing the total supply of schools.

Indian evidence (Muralidharan and Sundararaman 2015) suggests that private schools are more productive than public schools (delivering similar or modest improvements in learning at a much lower cost per child). Thus, if privately managed schools (with autonomy over teacher hiring, retention, pay and performance management) were to have the same level of per-child spending as the current government schooling system, we could potentially substantially improve learning outcomes without increasing the spending per child from the status quo (although there is no direct evidence of this to date). There are hundreds of high-quality operators of private schools who would be willing to operate hundreds or thousands of new schools (or take on management contracts of existing government schools) that serve EWS students if offered a reliable per-child compensation by the government that is of similar magnitude to the current spending per child in government schools.

Of course, leveraging such operators for providing a public interest good like education will require adequate oversight and regulation. But an enabling framework for such an approach could put India on a qualitatively different path for improving education outcomes in the coming decade. At the very least, policy guidelines to this effect can motivate serious pilots and evaluations of this approach.

7. **Taking vocational education seriously:** The jobs crisis in India is partly a skills crisis with millions of 'educated' unemployed youth on the one hand and employers routinely complaining that they cannot find adequately skilled manpower. A major reason for this is the focus of the education system on passing exams (usually by cramming) with no real understanding of the subject matter.

While there is not enough research on vocational education in India to have evidence-backed ideas for policy, there is suggestive evidence from the United States of the importance of integrating vocational education into secondary and higher secondary school curricula. Recent research suggests that the rising 'college wage premium' (defined as the wage increase of a college graduate relative to a high school one) may not be being driven only by a more complex economy and the greater need for higher education (as is commonly believed). Rather, it suggests that this may be explained at least in part by changes in high school curricula. Specifically, Alon (2018) shows that high school curricula in the United States used to have substantial vocational content up to the 1950s but that this changed in the 1960s to focus almost exclusively on college preparation.

While this made sense for students who did go to college, it may have worsened labour market outcomes for those who did not – since their high school education did not suitably prepare them for the labour market (compared to previous curricula that had more vocational content).

It is important for India not to repeat this mistake. Vocational education is widely seen as not desirable and something that is only chosen by students who are not academically smart. This will have to change if we are to provide the human capital needed to enable inclusive growth.

Some of the leading education systems in the world, including those in Singapore, Germany and Switzerland, feature tracking of students into vocational streams after grades six or seven. This allows these students to obtain more human capital than they would obtain by staying in school, through a combination of vocational classroom training and practical training or apprenticeships. The training is also linked to credible credentialing (which is sorely missing in our current skills ecosystem). This enables markets to pay a wage premium for skills, and qualified workers in technical fields can earn middle-class wages and incomes.

India would do well to think seriously about such an approach, which would likely better serve the millions of students who 'pass' exams but cannot find jobs because they have no real skills.

Appendix A: Heterogeneity and Learning Levels in Middle and Primary Grades

The figures on pages 161 and 163 show the levels and dispersion of student achievement in mathematics and Hindi in samples of students from two states, Delhi and Rajasthan. This comes from two separate studies using the Mindspark software (developed by Educational Initiatives, an Ahmedabad-based company) with government school students in these states.

The graphs rely on two pieces of information: (a) the grade that students are enrolled in and (b) the software's assessment, based on a common diagnostic test given to all students at the beginning of the intervention which assesses their actual ability levels. This can be thought of as the software's assessment (based on all questions answered) of the achievement level of the child (and is the level at which the software will begin to pitch instruction afterwards).

Figures 1 and 2 come from a sample of students from five government schools in Delhi who had chosen to take part in an evaluation study of Mindspark and had been selected randomly by lottery (and are reproduced from Muralidharan, Singh, and Ganimian 2017).

Note that the main reason these data rely on computer-based assessments is that the tests are administered without

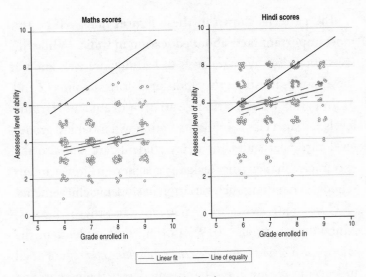

Figures 1 and 2: Learning levels in Delhi schools

ceiling or floor effects. This dynamic testing allows us to measure the exact learning level of each student. In contrast, paper-and-pencil tests (typically of grade-level content) suffer from severe floor effects in the Indian context. Thus, if a student has a very low score on such a test, we have no idea as to *how far below* grade-appropriate competence the student is (whereas this is not a problem on a dynamic computer-based test).

There are three key patterns illustrated by these figures:

1. By the beginning of grade 6, students are, on average, 2.5 years behind in maths.
2. By grade 9, this gap is even larger, at about 4.5 years in maths and 2.5 in Hindi.
3. In any given grade, the learning levels of students span four or five grade levels.

The patterns shown in these figures may well be the most important facts about education in India. While the facts about low average levels of learning are well known, these figures illustrate two additional critical points (2 and 3). In particular, the striking variation in student learning levels *within* a class highlights both how far behind grade-level curricular standards many students are and also the extremely challenging task for teachers in government schools in handling such variation in student achievements.

Consistent with the patterns in these figures, Muralidharan, et al. (2019) also find that students in the *lowest third of within-grade test scores make no progress* at all in learning during the school year, despite being enrolled in and attending school (consistent with their being so far behind curricular standards that textbook-based classroom instruction is essentially useless).

These facts are implied by several other studies across India as well, and are likely to be an important reason for why the very large increases in education expenditure and resources in the past two decades have not translated into improved learning (because these resources do not address the binding constraint of the education system, which is that children are too far behind).

One limitation of Figures 1 and 2 is that the sample is limited, coming only from five schools in one city and, further, from a non-representative set of students who chose to be part of the study.

Figures 3 and 4 draw instead on a much larger sample of over 5000 students in forty Adarsh schools in four districts in Rajasthan, covering both urban and rural areas and spanning the entire range of elementary school from

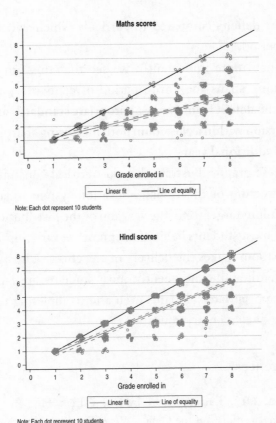

Figures 3 and 4: Learning levels in Rajasthan Adarsh schools

classes one to eight (from an ongoing study of the impacts of deploying the Mindspark software in government schools in Rajasthan).

All students in these classes in the programme schools were covered (and hence we do not need to worry about self-selection of better/worse performing students here). As we can see, the entire pattern observed in the smaller sample in Delhi is evident in Rajasthan too: there is similar dispersion in classes six to eight as in Delhi, and similar deficits compared to curricula which widen over this period.[7]

Much more importantly, we see that this process of widening spans the entire period of elementary school with the **deficit from grade-appropriate standards and the dispersion within a classroom both increasing sharply with every additional year.**

These graphs illustrate the most critical constraints in the structure of the Indian education system today: the curriculum targets only the very top of the distribution and leaves most students behind; the immense variation within a classroom makes the delivery of any effective instruction very hard; and, consequently, most students are far from class-appropriate standards even after completing the full course of elementary education.

References

T. Alon, 2018, 'Earning More by Doing Less: Human Capital Specialization and the College Wage Premium', Northwestern University.

A. Banerjee, S. Cole, E. Duflo, and L. Linden, 2007, 'Remedying Education: Evidence from Two Randomized Experiments in India', *Quarterly Journal of Economics*, 122: 1235–64.

A. Banerjee., R. Banerji, J. Berry, E. Duflo, H. Kannan, S. Mukerji, M. Shotland, and M. Walton, 2017, 'From Proof of Concept to

---

[7] The one change is that there are now no students assessed at above grade level (unlike in Hindi in Delhi). This is an artefact of the algorithm which was modified in 2017 to cap assessed student achievement at their current grade (since the primary purpose of this metric is to fix the level at which instruction will be presented to students).

Scalable Policies: Challenges and Solutions, with an Application', *Journal of Economic Perspectives*, 31: 73–102.

FICCI and Ernst & Young, 2014, 'Private Sector's Contribution to K-12 Education in India: Current Impact, Challenges, and Way Forward'.

G. Kingdon and F. Teal, 2010, 'Teacher Unions, Teacher Pay and Student Performance in India: A Pupil Fixed Effects Approach', *Journal of Development Economics*, 91: 278–88.

K. Muralidharan, 2012, 'Long Term Effects of Teacher Performance Pay: Experimental Evidence from India', University of California, San Diego.

——, 2013, 'Priorities for Primary Education Policy in India's 12th Five-Year Plan', *India Policy Forum*, 9: 1–46.

——, 2016, 'A New Approach to Public Sector Hiring in India for Improved Service Delivery', *India Policy Forum*.

K. Muralidharan, A. Singh, and A. Ganimian, 2019, 'Disrupting Education? Experimental Evidence on Technology-Aided Instruction in India', *American Economic Review*.

K. Muralidharan and V. Sundararaman, 2011, 'Teacher Performance Pay: Experimental Evidence from India', *Journal of Political Economy*, 119: 39–77.

——, 2015, 'The Aggregate Effects of School Choice: Evidence from a Two-Stage Experiment', *Quarterly Journal of Economics*, 130: 1011–66.

Joppe de Ree, Karthik Muralidharan, Menno Pradhan, and Halsey Rogers, 2018, 'Double for Nothing? Experimental Evidence on an Unconditional Teacher Salary Increase in Indonesia', *The Quarterly Journal of Economics*, 133(2): 993–1039.

The Solutions

1. A national mission to ensure, by 2022, that every child can actually read, write and do simple maths by the time they have finished class three. For this, hire part-time primary school teachers – trainees or even high-school students – to focus on those being left behind.

2. Introduce universal preschool, perhaps through anganwadi childcare centres. This will ensure that children from families receiving formal education for the first time do not start at a disadvantage that grows with time.

3. Change how teachers are trained, by increasing the emphasis on practical, hands-on experience.

4. Reform the RTE so that private schools can be supported and focus on the educational outcomes they deliver rather than on a rigid set of requirements for schools. Also change high school education to introduce a strong vocational education and apprenticeship track.

11

WOMEN AND WORK

The Problems

1. Not only do too few women work in India, but the proportion of women outside the labour force is increasing – and fast.
2. Even in high-skill professions like engineering and management, the proportion of women working is falling – although women are increasingly better educated. This suggests discrimination against women is not just all-pervasive but increasing over time.
3. Even those women that work are concentrated in 'traditional' professions, such as domestic work or teaching.
4. Existing skilling and employment generation programmes ignore the additional constraints on women workers – which means that they stay disadvantaged.

Building an Inclusive Labour Force

Rohini Pande

Key challenges and concerns

Higher labour market barriers for socially and economically disadvantaged population groups can increase the transmission of disadvantage across generations. This note summarizes the key challenges and concerns faced by one group – women – and discusses a few policy options.

Low rates of job creation, an increasing capital–labour ratio and lack of jobs for the highly skilled are leading to growing unemployment in India.[1] For the employed, wage growth has remained low.[2] The weight of both is felt more

---

[1] Between 2011 and 2016 the Indian workforce (those in work or actively seeking employment) grew at a low rate of approximately 2.5 per cent per annum – reaching 934 million (Basole, et al. 2018). Household surveys such as the National Sample Survey and Labour Bureau's survey are used to calculate the unemployment and labour force participation rates. See data sources in bibliography.

[2] The majority of households have an income below the Seventh Central Pay Commission level, leading to excessive demand for government jobs: 82 per cent of male and 92 per cent of female workers earn less than Rs 10,000 a month (minimum salary recommended by the Seventh Central Pay Commission is Rs 18,000 (Basole, et al. 2018).

by women and other marginalized groups. India's female labour force participation (FLFP) rate is low and has been falling precipitously. National Sample Surveys (NSS) show that between 1983 and 2011, Indian married women's labour force participation (LFP) declined from 35 per cent to 24 per cent, even while the economy grew, educational attainment rose and fertility fell. By 2015, according to the Labour Bureau (LB), only 23 per cent of working age women were in the labour force.[3]

Worryingly, these declines are visible in high skill professions: the percentage of female employees among high-return professions (senior officers, legislators and managers) fell from 13 per cent in 2011 to 7 per cent in 2015 (Basole, et al. 2018). Among engineers, the unemployment rate for women is five times that for men (Goel, 2007; Patel and Parmentier, 2005). Nationally, the unemployment rate for women engineers in India is about 40 per cent (Anand 2016). And while women constituted just over 22 per cent of the manufacturing workforce in 2015, they made up only 16 per cent of workers in the service sector. Tellingly, women's share in a service industry exceeded this number only in industries that extend their traditional household responsibilities: education (39 per cent), health (46 per cent) and domestic services (59 per cent).

Low FLFP in India is accompanied by:

---

[3] More recent estimates are highly variable. The Centre for Monitoring Indian Economy enumerated FLFP in 2017 at 12 per cent. The ILO estimate was 27 per cent in the same year. Even at the latter, more optimistic figure, India ranked 121 out of 131 countries for FLFP.

- Marginalization among the unemployed; the vast majority of those outside the labour force but willing to work are women.
- Concentration of women in low-paying or socially acceptable industries – in essence, those that are a formal extension of domestic or childcare work.
- Higher share of household duties and childcare, irrespective of employment status.

An important driver of these trends is sex-based discrimination. Mondal, et al. (2018) show the gender wage gaps were primarily explained by discrimination (i.e., after accounting for different skill endowments between men and women) from 1993 to 2011 and **increased** in the same time period. Deshpande, Goel, and Khanna (2018) corroborate these findings and conclude that, given the improvement in education for women over the decade from 2000, if women's endowments were valued equal to men's then the wage gap would have **reversed** by now. So, how should policy respond to these trends?

Labour market reforms: Recommendations

Over the years, Indian state and Central governments have made multiple labour market reforms that target women. We recommend building on this body of reforms, while ensuring that any strengthening of existing reforms is undertaken in a manner that avoids unanticipated perverse effects. We discuss four different reform categories.

Strengthening existing policy: Affirmative action in employment could mimic the success of reservation policies for caste and women in politics, but better monitoring is required.

- Indian Central and state governments often use reservation policies in public administration and politics to increase representation. Reservation policies increased SC/ST representation in regular salaried employment by around five percentage points (Borooah, Dubey, and Iyer 2007). Fletcher, Moore, and Pande (2018) note the significant rise in female employment in education after Operation Blackboard effectively reserved teacher positions for women. Evidence from panchayats, where reservation for women has existed for a significant period, suggests that quotas can also reduce bias against women (Beaman, et al. 2009).

- Some states are experimenting with broad-based gender quotas for public sector employment (e.g., Rajasthan introduced a 30 per cent reservation for women in government jobs in 2010 including a 5 per cent reservation for widows) and other states have targeted quotas in specific sectors (e.g., police in Gujarat).

- More attention needs to be given to:
  - Monitoring whether these quotas are filled, and necessary complementary policies to skill women in the required fields.
  - In terms of skilling, a survey of vocational trainees in 2016 found that female quotas in training can act as ceilings to FLFP in some cases, indicating the

policy may not reduce bias in the long term (Artiz Prillaman, et al. 2017). Here, it will be important to actively reduce explicit and implicit bias among trainers and recruiters.

Redesigning policy strategy: Increase social programmes that target individuals rather than households and ensure effective implementation

- The social causes of gender discrimination are insidious. The most challenging include the stigma against women working (particularly when married and/or with children) and migrating (except for marriage). A woman working outside the home drains household status in an extremely patriarchal society (Bernhardt, et al. 2018).
- Additionally, in patriarchal and patrilineal societies, household work is deemed the domain of women. This affects women throughout their lives – as daughters and eventually as wives. Unsurprisingly, marriage and having children are particularly highly correlated with women leaving the workforce (Jayachandran 2015). Changing norms thus requires intervening within the household.
- Direct benefits transfers are an increasingly important part of India's social sector infrastructure. Currently, political parties are stating interest in targeted minimum income programmes. It is important that they also discuss who in the household will receive the transfers. Research suggests value to transferring these resources to women's accounts (Field, et al. 2019).

*Changing policy approach: Mainstream gender in
labour market policies*

- Policies to increase FLFP are often considered separately
  from those of job creation and skilling. This can mean
  FLFP programmes fail to level the playing field. For
  example, skilling programmes in India are usually blind
  to the different safety and mobility concerns of men
  and women. Gender quotas in programmes like this are
  valuable, but likely to fail if the programme does not
  account for gender-based labour market barriers (Artiz
  Prillaman, et al. 2017).
- Skilling programmes should explicitly account for
  mobility barriers faced by women and their safety
  concerns. Migration support centres can play an
  important role.

*Influencing the private sector: Subsidize the cost to
employers of women-friendly policies*

- There are important efficiency reasons for increasing
  female employment. However, it is likely that the social
  benefits exceed the private benefits.
- As such, firms may not have incentives to support
  policies that would benefit governments and society at
  large. A classic example is India's recent maternity leave
  policy, where the cost is borne by private firms. Initial
  figures since the passage of the bill suggest that firms
  may be responding to higher costs by lowering female

employment.[4] Tax benefits, amnesty or similar schemes could align public and private sector incentives for hiring women.

- We propose immediate government funding for paid maternity leave with a focus on less-educated women and those in casual employment. The sentiment that women are 'costly' employees given employer-paid maternity leave is not unique to India: a 2014 survey of managers in the United Kingdom found that 40 per cent avoided hiring women as the costs of maternity leave were 'too high'.[5] For evidence in favour of government-funded maternity leave we refer to two cases and propose two specific reforms:

  - First, we consider an experiment in California. In 2002, California passed the first comprehensive paid family leave (PFL) programme in the United States. The programme provides six weeks of partial wage replacement for workers who go on leave to bond with a new biological, adopted or foster child.[6] The programme is funded by an employee-paid, inflation-indexed payroll tax, meaning there are no direct costs

---

[4] TeamLease (2018) Maternity Report suggests between 1.1 million and 1.8 million **fewer** women across 10 sectors will achieve employment in 2018–19 because of the Maternity Leave Act. Extrapolating to all sectors raises the figure to around 12 million.

[5] See https://www.theguardian.com/money/2014/aug/12/managers-avoid-hiring-younger-women-maternity-leave

[6] For birth mothers, this is available in addition to medical leave offered to recover from pregnancy and childbirth.

to employers. It is linked to California's existing state disability insurance (SDI) system, such that the administrative burden does not fall on businesses.

– Second, we consider the Australian government's parental pay leave (PPL). This is a government-funded scheme giving up to eighteen weeks of pay at the national minimum wage to full-time, part-time and casual working mothers.[7] The payments are made to the employer first, who then pays them to the employee. New mothers can claim PPL or receive paid parental leave from their employer.

Within any policy or legislation on this issue, it is important to protect new mothers' jobs with legislative guarantees that prevent employers from filling the positions of women on maternity leave.

Bibliography

Cinthya Anand, 2016, 'Number of Unemployed Women Engineers in India Is as High as 40 Per Cent', *The Hindu*, 26 August 2016.

E. Applebaum and R. Milkman, 2011, 'Paid Family Leave Pays Off in California', *Harvard Business Review*, https://hbr.org/2011/01/paid-family-leave-pays-off-in, accessed 15 October 2018.

——, 2011, 'Leaves that Pay: Employer and Worker Experiences with Paid Family Leave in California',

---

[7] For more details, see: https://www.fairwork.gov.au/leave/maternity-and-parental-leave/paid-parental-leave

http://cepr.net/documents/publications/paid-family-leave-1-2011.pdf, accessed 15 October 2018.

Soledad Artiz Prillaman, Rohini Pande, Vartika Singh, and Charity Troyer Moore, 2017, 'What Constrains Young Indian Women's Labor Force Participation? Evidence from a Survey of Vocational Trainees', Evidence for Policy Design: Harvard University.

Amit Basole, et al., 2018, State of Working India 2018, Azim Premji University, Bengaluru.

Lori Beaman, Raghabendra Chattopadhyay, Esther Duflo, Rohini Panda, and Petia Topalova, 2009, 'Powerful Women: Does Exposure Reduce Bias?' *Quarterly Journal of Economics*, 124(4): 1497–540.

Marianne Bertrand and Sendhil Mullainathan, 2004, 'Are Emily and Greg More Employable than Lakisha and Jamal? A Field Experiment on Labour Market Discrimination', *American Economic Review*, 94(4): 991–1013.

Arielle Bernhardt, Erica Field, Rohini Pande, Natalia Rigol, Simone Schaner, and Charity Troyer Moore, 2018, 'Male Social Status and Women's Work', American Economic Association: Papers & Proceedings, 108, pp. 363–67.

Vani K. Borooah, Amaresh Dubey, and Sriya Iyer, 2007, 'The Effectiveness of Jobs Reservation: Caste, Religion and Economic Status in India', *Development and Change*, 38(3): 423–45.

Ashwini Deshpande, Deepti Goel, and Shantanu Khanna, 2018, 'Bad Karma or Discrimination? Male–Female Wage Gaps among Salaried Workers in India', *World Development*, 102: 331–44.

Rachel Glennerster, Claire Walsh, and Lucia Diaz-Martin,

2018, 'A Practical Guide to Measuring Women's and Girls' Empowerment in Impact Evaluations', JPAL.

S. Goel, 2007, 'Women in Engineering in India', *The International Journal of Interdisciplinary Social Sciences: Annual Review*, 1(6): 1833–82.

Institute for Social Sciences Research, University of Queensland, 2014, PPL Evaluation: Final Report.

Seema Jayachandran, 2015, 'The Roots of Gender Inequality in Developing Countries', *Annual Review of Economics*, 7: 63–88.

S. Madheswaran and Smrutirekha Singhari, 2016, 'Social Exclusion and Caste Discrimination in Public and Private Sectors in India: A Decomposition Analysis', *Indian Journal of Labour Economics*, 59(2): 175–201.

Santosh Mehrotra, 2018, 'The Indian Labour Market: A Fallacy, Two Looming Crises and a Tragedy', SWI Background Paper 2018–9, Azim Premji University, Bengaluru.

Bidisha Mondal, Jayati Ghosh, Shiney Chakraborty, and Sona Mitra, 2018, 'Women Workers in India: Labour Force Trends, Occupational Diversification and Wage Gaps'. SWI Background Paper 2018–3, Azim Premji University, Bengaluru.

NITI Aayog, 2017, 'Report of the Task Force on Improving Employment Data', National Institution for Transforming India, New Delhi, http//niti.gov.in/content/report-taskforce-improving-employment-data#.

Uma Rani and Jeemol Unni, 2009, 'Do Economic Reforms Influence Home-Based Work? Evidence from India', *Feminist Economics*, 15(3): 191–225.

TeamLease, 2018, 'Maternity Report', http://www.

teamleasegroup.com/maternity-report, accessed on 7 October 2018.

Sukhadeo Thorat and Paul Attewell, 2007, 'The Legacy of Social Exclusion: A Correspondence Study of Job Discrimination in India', *Economic and Political Weekly*, 42(41): 4141–45.

Data sources (Basole, et al. 2018)

Quinquennial Employment-Unemployment Surveys of the NSSO (NSS-EUS): 1993–94 to 2011–12.

Annual Employment-Unemployment Surveys of the Labour Bureau (LB-EUS): 2nd Round (2011–12) and 5th Round (2015–16).

Centre for Monitoring Indian Economy (CMIE): The CMIE, in collaboration with the Bombay Stock Exchange, has been publishing reports called 'Unemployment in India: A Statistical Profile' since 2016. Three reports are published per year.

International Labour Organization statistical database (ILO-STAT).

The Solutions

1. Quotas for women might help, and there is clear evidence that they have reduced bias; but they need to be carefully monitored to make sure they are effective.
2. Because of ingrained patriarchy, the government may have to start intervening in how households operate – for example, by ensuring that income transfers under various schemes go to the woman's bank account.
3. Gender sensitivity and women workers' specific needs should be built into the design of all employment and skilling schemes. For example, safe transport to and from the workplace needs to be a priority.
4. The social benefits from more women working are high enough that this may be a fit case for subsidies to change the incentives of the private sector. For example, total or partial state funding for maternity leave has been shown to be helpful.

12

THE FINANCIAL SECTOR

The Problems

1. Indian companies depend too much on borrowing from banks to finance their investment. They need to be able to access a corporate bond market as an additional source of credit.

2. Banks are forced to spend some of their capital on government debt through the statutory liquidity ratio (SLR). The government uses this to tap household savings to finance its fiscal deficit. But it means that there is less room available for corporate bonds.

3. The government's reliance on banks to hold its securities means that individuals and foreign investors find it difficult to access safe and secure sovereign-guaranteed returns.

4. While many Indians now have a bank account, trust in – and understanding of – the formal financial sector still has to be built to encourage households to save financially rather than through, say, buying gold.

Financial Sector Development and Reforms*

Eswar Prasad

To sustain India's high growth rate and spread its benefits more evenly, the financial sector has a crucial role to play in mobilizing resources and channelling them to productive uses.

A well-developed financial system should effectively harness domestic savings; facilitate the efficient allocation of domestic and foreign savings to productive investments; allow households and firms to share risk; and support consumption and expenditure smoothing. To meet these goals, the financial sector needs a strong banking system as well as deep equity and bond markets. These in turn should be supported by liquid secondary markets and a robust regulatory and legal infrastructure.

Financial sector development should go hand-in-hand with reducing inequality in access to finance, with the aim

---

* This note draws extensively on Isha Agarwal and Eswar Prasad, 'A Vision and Action Plan for Financial Sector Development and Reforms in India', 2018, Brookings Institution Report.

of achieving universal coverage of banking and financial services.

The long-term objectives of financial sector reforms include the following:

- Making the banking system more robust and well capitalized, expanding its capacity to extend credit and improving incentives to lend to the most productive sectors.
- Increasing the reach of banking services with the aim of achieving universal coverage.
- Developing a liquid and deep corporate bond market to enable firms to raise debt at a low cost, with a view to gradually increasing the share of corporate bond markets in the financing of firms and providing an alternative to bank financing.
- Enhancing liquidity in the government debt market and making it more attractive to institutional and retail investors.
- Developing missing (or nascent) markets like fixed income derivatives to hedge the credit and interest rate risk of fixed income securities.
- Integrating financial markets, streamlining regulation, eliminating regulatory arbitrage.
- Creating a robust legal framework and effective judicial apparatus that supports the functioning of financial markets.
- Developing sophisticated IT infrastructure for trading exchanges that has the capability to support trading of innovative financial products.
- Making the financial sector more open to international investment to enable India to become a global financial centre in the long term.

Some specific recommendations regarding different parts of the financial system follow below.

Corporate bond markets

- **Increase the participation of institutional investors in the corporate bond market by relaxing norms on investment guidelines.** There are restrictions on institutional investors such as insurance companies and pension funds that inhibit their demand for corporate bonds. Relaxing these limits can help increase the participation in the Indian corporate bond market of these big-ticket, long-term investors.

- **Reduce the Statutory Liquidity Ratio.** The SLR determines how much government debt banks are forced to hold. A reduction in the SLR would allow banks to instead increase their holding of corporate bonds. The RBI has initiated the process of reducing the SLR; implementing a clear medium-term path for bringing down the SLR significantly would help banks prepare better, increase depth and liquidity in bond markets and reduce financial system distortions resulting from bank financing of fiscal deficits through their holdings of government debt.

- **Develop the credit-default swap (CDS) market for corporate bonds to help investors hedge risk.** Investment in corporate bonds is risky. Investors will be more willing to invest in the bond market if they have access to a CDS market in which they can hedge their risk. The RBI should allow netting of exposures to make trading in CDSs less expensive, while retaining regulatory safeguards to prevent excessive gross exposures.

Restrictions preventing institutional investors from selling CDSs should be removed, and foreign investors could be allowed to sell CDS contracts.

- **Rationalize stamp duty.** Rationalization of stamp duty can make bond issuance more attractive – but action on this suggestion, first proposed in the R.H. Patil Committee Report (2005), has been slow. The government should take prompt action on this reform.

- **Increase the limit on foreign portfolio investment.** The current limit on foreign investment in corporate bonds accounts for less than 10 per cent of the value of outstanding corporate bonds. The RBI should consider increasing this limit. Higher foreign investment will not only bolster the liquidity of the market but will also improve market discipline.

- **Creation of a benchmark yield curve.** Government securities (G-Secs) set the benchmark yields for the corporate bond markets. In India, G-Secs issued tend to be of longer duration – i.e., they are concentrated in the long end of the yield curve. Hence, there is no reliable benchmark yield for the short end of the yield curve. This makes pricing of corporate bonds difficult. Expanding the G-Sec market to include bonds with short maturities will help develop a benchmark yield curve for corporate bonds, which are clustered in the short-medium tenor (up to five years).

Government bond markets

- **Increase diversity in the investor base in the G-Sec market.** The share of scheduled commercial banks in the investor base should be gradually brought down by lowering the SLR. The market should also be made more accessible to retail investors. Foreign investment in the G-Sec market is low and can be increased to add diversity to the investor base. Rupee-denominated bonds do not carry currency risk. Global investors are likely to find the masala bond market attractive, given the positive growth outlook for the Indian economy and low interest rates in advanced economies.

- **Increase issuance of inflation-indexed bonds and floating-rate bonds.** These instruments are attractive to investors and provide a measure of inflation expectations, which helps guide monetary policy. In addition, they will encourage fiscal discipline by making inflation costly for the government, thereby serving as a commitment device for maintaining low inflation.

Other financial markets

- **Increase retail participation in the equity market.** Implement measures to increase the low retail participation in equity markets in India and mobilize the large pool of household savings through these markets, perhaps by educating people about the benefits (and risks) of investing in them. Eliminating regulatory arbitrage and increasing the ease of investment can also increase investor participation in the equity market.
- **Initiate steps to reduce market concentration in equity markets.** On the supply side, participation of smaller firms should be encouraged to make the market less concentrated. One way is to reduce entry costs for small

firms. To bolster demand for shares issued by small firms, tax incentives can be given to investors for investment in small- or mid-cap firms.

- **Restore confidence of market participants in the commodities market.** This can be done by minimizing ad hoc government interference and strengthening measures to detect market abuse.
- **Improve liquidity in the commodities derivatives market.** Remove restrictions on the participation of banks, mutual funds, institutional investors and foreign investors in the commodities derivatives market.
- **Introduce more hedging instruments for commodities.** Trading in commodities is inherently risky, partly because commodity prices are determined internationally and also because they are influenced by both domestic and global factors. Hence, to improve liquidity in this market, there is a need to introduce more hedging instruments. The Securities and Exchange Board of India should allow options trading on a broad set of commodities.
- **Increase participation of farmers in trading of agricultural commodities.** Farmers' participation in these markets is limited, since the current procedures and guidelines are excessively complex. Having a demat or a trading account is a prerequisite to participate in the market. In addition to reducing procedural complexities, farmers should be given formal training on how to manage futures trading, perhaps by appointing special agents who can assist them in trading.
- **Develop the interest rate futures (IRF) market.** A major reason for low liquidity in this market is the limited retail participation in the government bond market,

which dampens demand for IRFs to hedge interest rate exposure. To increase participation in the IRF market, participation in the underlying G-Sec market should be made more diverse. Further, IRFs should be introduced on money market instruments that more closely track monetary policy changes.

- **Relax rules for foreign investment in exchange-traded IRFs.** Requirements that the gross short position in IRFs be less than the gross long position in G-Secs and IRFs may curtail foreign investment. Guidelines for investing in IRFs should be relaxed for foreign portfolio investors to make this market more liquid.

- **Increase participation of firms in the currency derivatives market by increasing open position limits.** While some degree of speculation may be required for the smooth functioning of the currency derivatives market, there should not be a huge disconnect between currency derivatives and the underlying market (foreign trade). Participation by firms to hedge currency risk can be encouraged by increasing open position limits for clients, which are lower than position limits for proprietary traders and stock brokers.

Financial inclusion

- **Complementing financial inclusion reforms with measures to improve financial literacy.** Having a bank account is a necessary but not a sufficient condition for people to rely on formal sources of finance. Trust has to be instilled in the local communities regarding the use of financial services. Banks should employ local staff in rural areas to provide doorstep knowledge about the use of financial services; local vendors should be given incentives to use their bank accounts to make transactions.

- **Shift away from saving in gold.** The majority of households invest their savings in gold, diverting a large pool of savings from the formal banking system. Incentives should be given to people to deposit their savings in bank accounts by offering attractive savings options. The government introduced sovereign gold bonds in 2015 but the market for these bonds has been thin. Making them available for sale on-tap (continuously, rather than in intermittent tranches) and reducing the lock-in period could boost demand.

- **Making the business correspondents (BCs) more reliable.** The BC model introduced by the RBI is a good approach to provide banking services in rural areas. The model needs to be made more reliable to restore trust of local communities in this programme. Agents should go through proper screening and be certified by the associated banks so that data security is not compromised. Grievance settlement centres should be made accessible to people in rural areas where cases of misappropriation of funds by BCs can be reported. A database on BCs would help to evaluate the effectiveness of this programme and assess the changes required.

- **Use of technology.** In 2015, according to World Bank data, 79 of every 100 persons in India had mobile cellular subscriptions. This implies that mobile banking can be used to a greater extent to provide banking services in the unbanked/underbanked areas, especially in remote areas where Internet connectivity is poor.

Regulation and supervision

- **Integration of financial markets.** Integration of trading will generate economies of scope and reduce trading costs, as participants will not need to maintain separate margins for separate trades. For instance, commodity exporters prone to price risk and currency risk now have to maintain two separate margins – one at the commodity exchange and the other at the securities exchange, which is inefficient and increases the cost of participating in the market.

- **Reforms on resolution of financial firms.** India does not have a well-defined resolution mechanism for failing financial firms. The draft bill on the resolution of financial firms should be pursued as a high priority to strengthen the legal landscape in India.

- **Effective implementation of the Insolvency and Bankruptcy Code:** The Insolvency and Bankruptcy Code (2016) is a welcome step in strengthening the legal infrastructure – but, as highlighted in Raghuram Rajan's note on banking reforms in this volume, effective implementation is crucial. Also, this cannot serve as a panacea for a broad range of corporate and banking sector deficiencies.

The Solutions

1. The government should expand, through deregulation, the market for corporate bonds. Long-term investors like pension funds and insurance companies should be encouraged to participate; the limits on foreign investors should also be relaxed.

2. Create a clear pathway to reducing the requirements for banks to hold government securities. Open up the government debt market to more foreign investors, as well as to individuals – who should be offered secure, inflation-indexed bonds.

3. Financial literacy needs to be built up, especially among those accessing formal finance for the first time. Mobile-first and rural-focused models for banking need to be developed to encourage people to shift their savings away from gold.

4. Both the regulatory and legal systems need to be strengthened. The Insolvency and Bankruptcy Code needs to be effectively implemented, and equivalent bankruptcy proceedings for financial firms need to be worked out.

13

BANKING REFORMS

The Problems

1. Indian banks – particularly public sector banks – are loaded down with non-performing loans. This means that they find it difficult to grow their new lending to industry, and growth suffers.
2. Cleaning up bad loans cannot be left entirely to the National Company Law Tribunal (NCLT), as that will quickly become clogged. But bankers worry that if they take bold decisions out of court then they will be subject to investigation.
3. Public sector banks are not professional enough. The government still controls appointments to their boards and their managements are short of talent and expertise.
4. Banks are forced to do too much and take on too much risk. Public sector banks have to bear the burden of government policy priorities such as loan waivers and directed lending. All banks suffer from the lack of well-developed financial markets that could take on some of the risk.

Banking Reforms

Raghuram Rajan

The banking system is overburdened with non-performing loans. Much of the problem lies in public sector banks, but private sector banks like ICICI and Axis Bank have not been immune. Some of the malaise comes from a general need to improve governance, transparency and incentives in the system. However, the difficulties in even some private banks suggest that 'simple' solutions like privatizing all public sector banks may be no panacea.

At any rate, banking reform should tackle four broad areas:

1. Clean up banks by reviving projects that can be revived after restructuring debt.
2. Improve governance and management at public sector banks.
3. De-risk banking by encouraging risk transfers to non-banks and the market.
4. Reduce the number and weight of government mandates for public sector banks, and for banks more generally.

Reviving projects that can be revived

The National Company Law Tribunal will help restructure debt for the largest firms and projects under the Bankruptcy Code. However, the NCLT will be overwhelmed if every stressed firm or project files before it. Instead, we need a functional out-of-court restructuring process, so that the vast majority of cases are restructured out of bankruptcy – with the NCLT acting as a court of last resort if no agreement is possible. Both the out-of-court restructuring process and the bankruptcy process need to be strengthened and made speedy. The former requires protecting the ability of bankers to make commercial decisions without subjecting them to inquiry. The latter requires steady modifications where necessary to the Bankruptcy Code so that it is effective, transparent, and not gamed by unscrupulous promoters.

Of course, for many projects, financial restructuring is of little use if the project cannot proceed for other reasons such as lack of land or permissions or input supply. Any new government will have to give priority to rectifying these issues. I will not go into details here since some of these bottlenecks are covered in other notes.

Improving governance and management at public sector banks

- Public sector bank boards are still not adequately professionalized, and the government rather than a more independent body still decides board appointments – with the inevitable politicization. The government could follow the P.J. Nayak Committee report more carefully.

Eventually strong boards should be entrusted with all bank-related decisions, including CEO appointment, but held responsible for performance. Strategic investors could help improve governance.

- Risk management still needs substantial improvement in public sector banks, regulatory compliance is inadequate and cyber risk needs greater attention. Interest rate risk management is notable for its absence, which means banks are very dependent on the central bank to smooth the path of long-term interest rates. These are all symptoms of managerial weakness. There is already a talent deficit in internal public sector bank candidates in coming years because of a hiatus in recruitment in the past. Outside talent has been brought in very limited ways into top management in public sector banks. This deficiency needs to be addressed urgently by searching more widely for talent. Compensation structures in public sector banks also need rethinking, especially for high-level outside hires.

Project lending has to be improved

- Significantly more in-house expertise can be brought to project evaluation and structuring, including understanding demand projections for the project's output, likely competition, and the expertise and reliability of the promoter. Bankers will have to develop industry knowledge in key areas or bring on board industry experts, since consultants can be biased.
- Real risks have to be mitigated where possible, and shared where not. Real risk mitigation requires ensuring that key

permissions for land acquisition and construction are in place up front, while key inputs and customers are tied up through purchase agreements. Government will have to deliver what it is responsible for in a timely way. Where these risks cannot be mitigated, they should be shared contractually between the promoter and financiers, or a transparent arbitration system should be agreed to.

- An appropriately flexible capital structure should be in place. The capital structure has to be related to residual risks of the project. The more the risks, the more the equity component should be (genuine promoter equity, not borrowed equity, of course), and the greater should be the flexibility in the debt structure.

- Where possible, corporate debt markets, either through direct issues or securitized project loan portfolios, should be used to absorb some of the initial project risk. More such arm's length debt should typically refinance bank debt when construction is over.

- Financiers should put in place a robust system of project monitoring and appraisal, including where possible, careful real-time monitoring of costs. Promoters should be incentivized to deliver, with significant rewards for on-time execution and debt repayment. Projects that are going off track should be restructured quickly, before they become unviable.

- And finally, the incentive structure for bankers should be worked out so that they evaluate, design and monitor projects carefully, and get significant rewards if these work out. Equally, bankers who preside over a series of bad projects should be identified and penalized.

Privatize or not?

Is privatization of public sector banks the answer? Much of the discussion on privatization seems to make assumptions based on ideological positions. Certainly, if public sector banks are freed from some of the constraints they operate under (such as paying above the private sector for low-skilled jobs and paying below the private sector for senior management positions, having to respond to government diktats on strategy or mandates, or operating under the threat of CVC/CBI scrutiny) they might perform far better. However, such freedom typically requires distance from the government. So long as they are majority-owned by the government, they may not get that distance.

At the same time, there is no guarantee that privatization will be a panacea. Some private banks have been poorly governed. Instead, we need to recognize that ownership is just one contributor to governance and look at pragmatic ways to improve governance across the board. There certainly is a case to experiment by privatizing one or two mid-sized public sector banks and reducing the government stake below 50 per cent for a couple of others, while working on governance reforms for the rest. Rather than continuing a never-ending theoretical debate, we will then actually have some evidence to go on. Some political compromises will be needed to allow the process to go through, but so long as the newly privatized banks are not totally hamstrung in their operational flexibility as a result of these compromises, this will be an experiment worth undertaking.

Merge or not?

An alternative proposal to improve governance is to merge poorly managed banks with good banks. It is uncertain whether this will improve collective performance – after all, mergers are difficult in the best of situations because of differences in culture. When combined with differences in management capabilities, much will depend on whether the good bank's management is strong enough to impose its will without alienating the employees of the poorly managed bank. We now have two experiments under way: State Bank has taken over its regional affiliates, and Bank of Baroda, Vijaya Bank and Dena Bank have been merged. The performance of the latter merger will be more informative. Thus far, market responses suggest scepticism that it will play out well. Time will tell.

De-risk banking by encouraging risk transfers to non-banks and the market

Too many risks devolve on to banks, including risks such as that of interest rate volatility that banks elsewhere typically lay off in markets. Too much project risk stays with banks because other financial instruments such as equity and subordinate debt cannot be issued cheaply. Risk also returns through the back door. For example, banks do not make loans to housing developers because of their intrinsic risks. But they do make loans to non-bank financial companies, which make loans to developers. To prevent risk from returning to bank balance sheets, NBFCs must be able to raise money directly from markets. Financial market development, addressed in Eswar Prasad's note in this volume, will help banks focus more on risks they can manage better and thus bear more effectively, while sharing or laying off what they cannot. Banks will have to complement financial markets rather than see them as competition. The use of financial technology will be especially helpful to them in this endeavour.

Reduce the number and weight of government mandates for public sector banks

Uncompensated government mandates have been imposed on public sector banks for a long time. This is lazy government – if an action is worth doing, it should be paid for out of budgetary resources. Mandates also are against the interests of minority shareholders in public sector banks. Finally, it does not draw the private sector in to compete for such activities. The government should incentivize all banks to take up activities it thinks desirable, not impose it on a few – especially as the privileges associated with a banking licence diminish.

Along these lines, requirements that banks mandatorily invest in government bonds (the SLR requirement) should continue to be reduced, substituting them instead with the liquidity coverage ratios and net stable funding ratios set by Basel.

Among the more dangerous mandates are lending targets and compulsory loan waivers. Government-imposed credit targets are often achieved by abandoning appropriate due diligence, creating the environment for future NPAs. Loan waivers, as the RBI has repeatedly argued, vitiate the credit culture and stress the budgets of the waiving state or Central government. They are poorly targeted, and eventually reduce the flow of credit. Agriculture needs serious attention, but not through loan waivers. An all-party agreement to this effect would be in the nation's interest.

Finally, the government should keep its banks well capitalized, conditional on improvements in governance and management efficiency. This is simply good accounting practice, for it prevents the government from building up contingent liabilities on bank balance sheets that a future government will have to pay for.

The Solutions

1. The P.J. Nayak Committee recommended a path to greater independence for public sector banks, and its ideas should be implemented. Eventually, public sector bank boards should be independent and accountable, and allowed to choose the banks' CEOs.
2. Banks need to build up more in-house talent for such specialized tasks as managing project finance. Public sector banks may have to start paying more to attract world-class talent.
3. Some mid-sized public sector banks should be privatized as a test case.
4. Banks should not be forced to implement the government's policy priorities. In particular, an all-party agreement that loan waivers should be avoided is in the national interest.

14

THE ENVIRONMENT AND CLIMATE CHANGE

The Problems

1. India is very vulnerable to climate change, with its agricultural and other productivity, health and water supply particularly at risk.
2. Existing environmental regulators are short of funding, capacity and power. They do not have enough scientists, depend upon politicians for their funding and do not have the right to set fees or fines.
3. Regulation that is either too lax or too harsh means that courts often intervene in environmental issues – sometimes levying excessive punishments or making excessive demands.
4. India's forest resources are inefficiently managed, with local communities having little say in how they are run. Stern rules about tree-cutting mean that too few new forests are created. There is little incentive to protect biodiversity and wildlife.

Environment

E. Somanathan

Pollution regulation

Air pollution has captured media attention recently, but it is a problem that has been building for many years. It is clear that our existing regulatory system failed to monitor the problem and intervene at a sufficiently early stage. But this is only one of many such looming problems. Water pollution in many places is equally serious. Not long ago, there were news reports that ammonia levels in the Yamuna river had become too high for purification plants to cope with. The fact is that our regulatory system is unable to perform the task of monitoring the environment and heading off threats before they become crises.

The problems with the existing legislation and regulatory system are:

- The central and state pollution control boards are underfunded and dependent on the political executive for their budget. They do not have autonomy in hiring and are understaffed – especially with regard to qualified scientific personnel. The Central Pollution Control

Board (CPCB) has a few hundred employees compared to 14,000 at the US Environmental Protection Agency, and the number of scientists is even fewer. There is no legal obligation to consider scientific evidence or conduct cost–benefit analyses.

- Only all-or-nothing penalties are available, so the choices facing the boards are effectively to either do nothing or shut down an industry. This has resulted in nothing being done until matters reach a crisis, when the courts intervene (sometimes in a draconian manner). The stop–go nature of regulation results in regulatory uncertainty, so that firms do not have appropriate incentives to invest in clean technology.

It is not possible to address major environmental problems in a cost-effective manner without making use of pollution fees or charges levied at the appropriate level (where the production chain is most concentrated), for example, a fee on plastic production at refineries (refunded if plastic is recovered, i.e., a fee on unrecycled plastic), since it is prohibitively costly to monitor small producers and retailers of plastic bags; a fee on fly ash or sulphur dioxide emitted by coal power plants; a fee on coal use (to cover small coal users whom it is not cost-effective to monitor individually); a fee on diesel at refineries (since it is not practical to monitor pollutants from individual vehicles); a fee on nitrogenous fertilizer use, since it is costly to monitor use on farms; and so on.

Recommendations for pollution regulation

Regulation should be delegated to an independent regulator at both the central and state levels, with the central regulator having overriding authority for all pollutants whose effects cross state boundaries. The existing regulatory structure should be enhanced in the following ways:

- The regulator should have the power to set and levy pollution fees on pollutants and on inputs that are closely related to pollutants. It should also have the power to levy fines for non-compliance with regulations or non-payment of fees.

- The regulator should be appointed for a five-year term, and not removable except by impeachment.

- The regulatory agency must be funded automatically through a charge on industry revenue, so that it is not dependent on annual budgetary appropriation. The charge must be set high enough to finance an authority with a budget that is comparable in terms of percentage of GDP to its developed-country counterparts. The budgetary increase should be phased in over a five-year period. The agency must have full autonomy for all its decisions including hiring and use of its budget.

- The regulator must be required to use the best available scientific and economic evidence to set pollution fees for pollutants (or inputs closely linked to pollutants) equal to the estimated monetary value of the harm that they cause, and to levy fines for non-compliance. Rules/fees and their justification must include a period for public comment before they are issued. All pollution monitoring data must be published without delay.

- The regulator must have the power to conduct and commission outside entities to conduct scientific (including economic) studies that may be used to determine appropriate regulations and fees.
- The regulator may **recommend** the use to which revenues from fees and fines may be put **but the ultimate decision in this regard must rest with the government** (state or Central as the case may be). Such revenues should not form part of the agency's budget.

Delegating the power to decide the appropriate level of regulation or fee to an independent scientific body is appropriate since the political system does not generate sufficient incentive to deal with problems that mature gradually and are difficult to understand. Giving the government the authority to determine the use of revenues generated from pollution charges is essential for appropriately compensating those adversely affected by regulation in a democratic manner. The scientific body is an inappropriate venue for final decisions involving distributional issues.

The regulator should have the power to issue quantitative limits on pollutants, or outright bans, in addition to being able to levy pollution fees.

Pollution fees have two great advantages. First, they induce an economically efficient reduction in pollution, because they offer inducements to all parties in production and consumption chains to change their behaviour to reduce pollution. For example, a fee on coal would raise the price of coal-fired electricity – which would in turn induce consumers to reduce wasteful uses and give appliance makers a better market for efficient appliances. It would also induce industries as diverse as brick kilns and power plants to upgrade their technologies to economize on the use of coal. And it would give a bigger market to renewable electricity generating technologies like wind and solar.

Second, they have a political advantage that is perhaps even more important. The present focus of industry lobbying is to stop regulations or water them down. With the existence of government revenue from pollution fees and a politically independent regulator, industry may conclude that lobbying the government to get a piece of the revenue from pollution fees in order to install pollution equipment or invest in clean alternatives will be more likely to yield fruit than lobbying to stop or delay regulations.

Not all pollution issues are amenable to remedy by such a regulator – for example, the household air pollution (HAP) problem. It is a common misunderstanding that HAP stays indoors. In fact, it is the single largest contributor to national air pollution. The cost-effective solution to HAP is to refund electricity bills for low-income households up to a limit like 100 kWh per month (higher in winter to allow for electric heat) and to charge them the same rate as other customers. This would greatly increase the existing market for induction stoves and take away most of the incentive to use solid fuels. It would also remove the existing incentive that distribution companies have to black out poor households that pay lower rates. Revenues could come from pollution fees levied by the regulator. This would be more cost-effective than subsidizing LPG, although it is likely that LPG will continue to be used in part until electricity supply reliability and quality improve.

Climate change

India is extremely vulnerable to climate change, and we have already suffered losses in terms of heat wave deaths (Mazdiyasni, et al. 2017), more damaging storms, yield losses of major crops (Auffhammer, et al. 2006; Gupta, et al. 2017), and productivity losses in the manufacturing sector (Somanathan, et al. 2015). However, the greatest dangers lie ahead. A recent assessment of changes in the Himalayas finds that up to 90 per cent of glacier ice could be lost by 2100 unless warming is reduced (Wester, et al. 2019, Figure 7.9). This would be catastrophic for water supply in North India in the non-monsoon months.

To a large degree, an effective pollution regulation system as outlined above will also reduce the emissions of greenhouse gases. The most important pollutant for global warming is carbon dioxide, produced by burning fossil fuels – coal, oil and gas. When fossil fuels are burnt, they produce other pollutants. Therefore, when pollution fees are levied on those pollutants, fossil fuel combustion and carbon dioxide emissions will also be discouraged.

Several complementary policies will be needed in addition – for example, the promotion of walking, cycling and public transport by providing appropriate urban infrastructure, and the electrification of transport by providing charging infrastructure. India also needs to adapt to that part of climate change that is now inevitable – by expanding research and development (R&D) of drought- and heat-sensitive crops, better flood planning and many other measures.

To hold the rise in global temperature to a safe level, the

world will have to stop adding to the quantity of carbon dioxide and greenhouse gases in the atmosphere, and eventually even move some from the air. However, India's share in global emissions of greenhouse gases is only about 7 per cent, fourth after China (26 per cent), the United States (15 per cent) and the EU (10 per cent). Getting these emissions down to zero in the next few decades – followed by negative emissions thereafter – will require a massive replacement of fossil fuels with renewables and other yet-to-be developed technologies. These will be developed if there is a ready market for them. That requires a rising price (once again, a pollution fee) of carbon emissions to induce R&D into all kinds of substitutes for fossil fuels. India should take the lead by proposing to the other large emitters that if they institute a rising carbon price with revenues to be retained domestically within each country, then India will match them. This will create pressure on them to take meaningful action.

Ecosystem protection

Forests and other natural ecosystems such as grasslands and wetlands outside the national park system are inefficiently managed by state forest departments (Somanathan, et al. 2009). Legislation is needed to hand over such lands, when they border villages, to local bodies such as gram sabhas to manage. This would result in more efficient management with higher production of timber and other forest products, and more afforestation (as suggested by the experience of Chinese forest reforms, Xu 2010). Gram sabhas would be efficient about timber production but may not do enough to protect wildlife and plant species diversity. Payments for ecosystem services financed by timber taxes would be more cost-effective and politically acceptable, when it comes to incentives for maintaining biodiversity and protecting wildlife, than existing regulations. An important aspect of such a reform would be the removal of existing laws and regulations that prohibit timber cutting and sales, even on private lands, so that farmers and local bodies have the incentive to plant trees.

The national park system should also be reformed to share revenues and management responsibility with local communities.

Legislation is needed to make the use of underpasses and overpasses mandatory for roads and railways. This will allow projects to go ahead without cutting off wildlife migration that is essential to prevent species from going extinct.

References

M. Auffhammer, V. Ramanathan, and J.R. Vincent, 2006, 'From the Cover: Integrated Model Shows That Atmospheric Brown Clouds and Greenhouse Gases Have Reduced Rice Harvests in India.' *Proceedings of the National Academy of Sciences*, 103(52): 19668–72.

Ridhima Gupta, E. Somanathan, and Sagnik Dey, 2017, 'Global Warming and Local Air Pollution Have Reduced Wheat Yields in India', *Climatic Change*, 140(3–4): 593–604.

O. Mazdiyasni, A. AghaKouchak, S.J. Davis, S. Madadgar, A. Mehran, E. Ragno, M. Sadegh, A. Sengupta, S. Ghosh, C.T. Dhanya, and M. Niknejad, 2017, 'Increasing

Probability of Mortality during Indian Heat Waves', *Science Advances*, 3(6):e1700066.

E. Somanathan, R. Prabhakar, and B.S. Mehta, 2009, 'Decentralization for Cost-Effective Conservation', *Proceedings of the National Academy of Sciences*, 106(11): 4143–47.

E. Somanathan, Rohini Somanathan, Anant Sudarshan, and Meenu Tewari, 2015, The Impact of Temperature on Productivity and Labor Supply: Evidence from Indian Manufacturing. Discussion Paper No. 15-03. Indian Statistical Institute, New Delhi, India.

P. Wester, A. Mishra, A. Mukherji, A.B. Shrestha, 2019, *The Hindu Kush Himalaya Assessment: Mountains, Climate Change, Sustainability and People*. Springer.

J.T. Xu, 2010, 'Collective Forest Tenure Reform in China: What Has Been Achieved So Far', In *World Bank Conference on Land Governance. World Bank, Washington, DC*, http://policydialogue.org/files/events/XuJintao_collective_forest_tenure_reform_china.pdf.

The Solutions

1. An independent regulator in every state and at the Centre should be created that is funded directly through a charge on industry. This regulator should be able to use scientific evidence to set pollution fees and fines, so that incentives change through the entire supply chain of a polluting industry.

2. Households should be encouraged to switch to electricity for activities like cooking – in particular, through a refund of the power bill of low-income households. People should be given the incentive to switch to electric vehicles by rolling out charging infrastructure nationwide.

3. India's global strategy on climate change should focus on an acceptance of the idea of a higher price on carbon, which will induce greater research into substitutes for fossil fuels.

4. Local communities should be given greater control over forest resources, alongside payments for maintaining the ecosystem of forested areas.

AFTERWORD
Eight Challenges and Eight Reforms*

Abhijit Banerjee and Raghuram Rajan

In October 2018 thirteen of us, all economists, got together in the hope that, as the country gears up for elections, we could start a conversation by identifying a set of policy ideas that might help inform party manifestos and policy visions. While our views stretch across the spectrum from right to left, we found surprising agreement on the challenges India faces and reforms it needs now. Two of us sifted through the set of ideas, picking what we felt were the top challenges and proposals to address them.

As we see it, rethinking government is key. Government capacity is limited. We need to target it better while trying to enhance it. Stability in government policy is important so that our farmers and firms can plan better, and markets

---

* A version of this was first published in the *Times of India* on 1 January 2019.

can play a more effective role. Cooperative federalism –
Centre and states working together and learning from each
other – is essential.

Here are the eight top challenges India faces, and
proposals to deal with each:

1. The massive aggregate fiscal deficit of the states and the
    Centre combined leaves fewer, costlier, resources for
    private investment. We should aim to hit the FRBM-
    suggested 5 per cent of GDP by 2023 – but not through
    creative accounting or off-balance-sheet transactions.
    Instead, we must increase revenues, through both
    better compliance and more progressive taxation, and
    target spending better. State deficits have grown, partly
    because markets assume that the Centre will bail out
    overextended states and therefore do not charge them
    higher interest rates. To incentivize better behaviour,
    any state's borrowing above agreed limits should be
    funded through special bonds that are explicitly free of
    any federal guarantee. A Centre–state council modelled
    on the successful GST Council could supervise fiscal
    federalism.

2. Three sectors that are distressed today are agriculture,
    power and banking – despite massive past government
    intervention, and often because of it. For example,
    periodic export bans and large-scale imports to keep
    food inflation down have radically moved the terms of
    trade against agriculture, while reducing the farmer's
    ability to plan. Cheap or free power to farmers has
    depleted the water table to the point of disaster.
    Farmers do need assistance. However, the instruments
    used – loan waivers, inflated MSPs without adequate

procurement and input price subsidies – often exacerbate the problem. In addition to enhancing investment in new technologies and irrigation, a government move towards lump-sum payments to farmers with holdings below a certain limit, in the spirit of Telangana's Rythu Bandhu scheme, will be an improvement.

Similarly, distressed state-owned power distribution companies stand between power producers who want to sell more and consumers who want more reliable power. The solutions are well known – better metering, less distorted pricing of both power and energy inputs, and the use of new, cleaner technologies for distributed production and decentralizing distribution. All these require rethinking the government's role, as will any sustainable solution to banking sector distress.

3. We need a better business environment – whether to create the jobs for those leaving agriculture, urban schools or our universities, or to ramp up our woefully inadequate exports. We need to learn from states' experiences about what works in areas like land acquisition, industrial regulation, provision of power and logistics and environmental clearances. A Centre–state productivity council can be useful for this; such a council could revive the idea of special economic zones where coordinated land, environmental clearances and transportation infrastructure are available on a 'plug-in' basis. Such zones, not necessarily targeted at exports, may also be used to experiment with reforms such as changes in labour laws before an all-India rollout, to provide the evidence needed to build consensus for them.

4. Sustainable growth requires more effective but less burdensome regulation. Our cities are choking and climate change is upon us. Municipalities need the powers and funding to deal with these challenges, which means more decentralization. In other areas, we need more centralization: for instance, a new and technically beefed-up environmental regulator, combining powers that are currently with multiple bodies, setting fees based on careful analysis of trade-offs and enforcing them.

5. Government has to provide for benefits, but is not always best suited to deliver them. To reduce the implementation burden and free up its ability to take on new challenges, government should move towards cash transfers. As a first step, beneficiaries of all specific government subsidy programmes should have the choice between cash transfers and benefits in kind.

Many of our challenges also have to do with enhancing the capabilities of our people.

6. We need more skilled personnel in government – at higher levels in technical areas like digitization, trade negotiation and environmental regulation, but also at lower levels outside the larger cities. More lateral entrants, merging into the permanent civil service, are desirable near the top. At lower levels, too many young Indians waste years taking competitive exams for government jobs that most will never get. One alternative that will give them skills and work experience is a multi-year paid government internship at salaries comparable to entry-level market wages (much less than what the government pays) for those under twenty-six

to work as support staff in government offices or public sector enterprises where needed. Performance on these could help entry into permanent government jobs – though political pressure to make these internships permanent should be resisted.

7. The Right to Education Act focuses on input requirements for schools that have little bearing on learning outcomes, which have deteriorated alarmingly. Learning must be our central focus, with all schools, public and private, responsible for delivering a minimum level of basic skills to every child. Bringing those falling behind up to par through remedial teaching will be critical.

8. We must address the coming explosion of non-communicable diseases, which will require engagement with front line providers. The vast majority of these have no formal qualifications, but the evidence suggests they can be trained and pushed towards practising better medicine. Since they have the patients' ears, the health system should use them better rather than ignoring them.

Notes on the Editors and Contributors

Abhijit Banerjee is the Ford Foundation International Professor of Economics at the Massachusetts Institute of Technology and founded the Abdul Latif Jameel Poverty Action Lab (J-PAL).

Pranjul Bhandari is Chief India Economist at HSBC. She has earlier worked at the Union Ministry of Finance in New Delhi and Goldman Sachs in Hong Kong.

Sajjid Chinoy is Chief India Economist at JP Morgan, having previously been an Economist at the International Monetary Fund and a Senior Associate with McKinsey & Company in New York.

Maitreesh Ghatak is a Professor of Economics at the London School of Economics.

Gita Gopinath is Economic Counsellor and Director of Research at the International Monetary Fund.

Amartya Lahiri is Royal Bank Faculty Research Professor of Economics at the University of British Columbia and the Director of the Centre for Advanced Research and Learning.

Neelkanth Mishra is a Managing Director, co-head of Asia Pacific Strategy, and the India Economist and Strategist for Credit Suisse.

Prachi Mishra is the former head of the strategic research unit of the Reserve Bank of India and is currently Managing Director and Chief India Economist at Goldman Sachs.

Karthik Muralidharan is the Tata Chancellor's Professor of Economics at the University of California, San Diego.

Rohini Pande is the Rafik Hariri Professor of International Political Economy at Harvard Kennedy School.

Eswar Prasad is the Tolani Senior Professor of Trade Policy at Cornell University and a Senior Fellow at the Brookings Institution.

The former Governor of the Reserve Bank of India, Raghuram Rajan is an international academician and the Katherine Dusak Miller Distinguished Service Professor of Finance at University of Chicago Booth School of Business.

Mihir S. Sharma is Senior Fellow at the Observer Research Foundation and the head of its Economy and Growth Programme.

E. Somanathan is a Professor at the Economics and Planning Unit of the Indian Statistical Institute, Delhi.

juggernaut

THE APP
FOR INDIAN
READERS

*Fresh, original books tailored for
mobile and for India. Starting at ₹10.*

juggernaut.in

1

CRAFTED
FOR MOBILE
READING

*Thought you would never read a book
on mobile? Let us prove you wrong.*

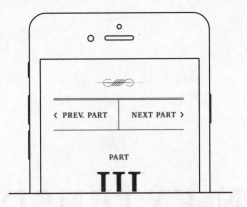

Beautiful Typography

The quality of print transferred
to your mobile. Forget ugly PDFs.

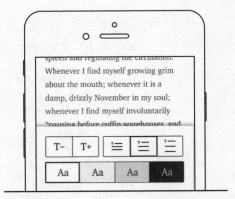

Customizable Reading

Read in the font size, spacing
and background of your liking.

AN EXTENSIVE LIBRARY

Including fresh, new, original Juggernaut books from the likes of Sunny Leone, Praveen Swami, Husain Haqqani, Umera Ahmed, Rujuta Diwekar and lots more. Plus, books from partner publishers and loads of free classics. Whichever genre you like, there's a book waiting for you.

DON'T JUST READ; INTERACT

We're changing the reading experience from passive to active.

Ask authors questions

Get all your answers from the horse's mouth.
Juggernaut authors actually reply to every
question they can.

Rate and review

Let everyone know of your favourite reads or
critique the finer points of a book – you will be
heard in a community of like-minded readers.

Gift books to friends

For a book-lover, there's no nicer gift than
a book personally picked. You can even
do it anonymously if you like.

Enjoy new book formats

Discover serials released in parts over
time, picture books including comics,
and story-bundles at discounted rates.
And coming soon, audiobooks.

4

LOWEST PRICES & ONE-TAP BUYING

Books start at ₹10 with regular discounts and free previews.

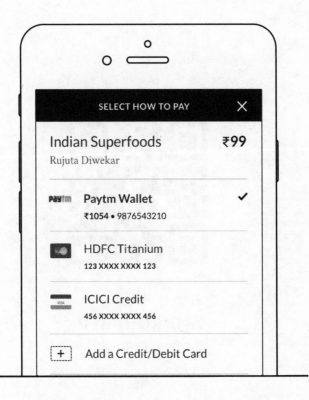

Paytm Wallet, Cards & Apple Payments

On Android, just add a Paytm Wallet once and buy any book with one tap. On iOS, pay with one tap with your iTunes-linked debit/credit card.

Click the QR Code with a QR scanner app
or type the link into the Internet browser
on your phone to download the app.

ANDROID APP
bit.ly/juggernautandroid

iOS APP
bit.ly/juggernautios

For our complete catalogue, visit www.juggernaut.in
To submit your book, send a synopsis and two
sample chapters to books@juggernaut.in
For all other queries, write to contact@juggernaut.in